HOW TO BUY
A HOUSE, CONDO,
OR CO-OP

HOW TO BUY
A HOUSE, CONDO, OR CO-OP

MICHAEL C. THOMSETT
AND THE
EDITORS OF CONSUMER REPORTS BOOKS

Consumers Union
Mount Vernon
New York

Special thanks to the following for their editing and reviewing help: Julie Henderson, Elias Zuckerman, Meryl Unger, Randy Amengual, and Steve Swiatkiewicz.

Copyright © 1987 by Michael C. Thomsett and Consumers Union of United States, Inc. Mount Vernon, New York 10553

Library of Congress Cataloging-in-Publication Data

Thomsett, Michael C.
  How to buy a house, condo, or co-op.

  Includes index.
  1. House buying. 2. Condominiums. 3. Apartment
houses, Cooperative. I. Consumer Reports Books.
II. Title.
HD1375.T534   1986   643'.12   86-2626
ISBN 0-89043-040-3

Third Printing, February 1988

Manufactured in the United States of America

How to Buy a House, Condo, or Co-op is a Consumer Reports Book published by Consumers Union, the nonprofit organization that publishes *Consumer Reports,* the monthly magazine of test reports, product Ratings, and buying guidance. Established in 1936, Consumers Union is chartered under the Not-For-Profit Corporation Law of the State of New York.

The purposes of Consumers Union, as stated in its charter, are to provide consumers with information and counsel on consumer goods and services, to give information on all matters relating to the expenditure of the family income, and to initiate and to cooperate with individual and group efforts seeking to create and maintain decent living standards.

Consumers Union derives its income solely from the sale of *Consumer Reports* and other publications. In addition, expenses of occasional public service efforts may be met, in part, by nonrestrictive, noncommercial contributions, grants, and fees. Consumers Union accepts no advertising or product samples and is not beholden in any way to any commercial interest. Its Ratings and reports are solely for the use of the readers of its publications. Neither the Ratings nor the reports nor any Consumers Union publications, including this book, may be used in advertising or for any commercial purpose. Consumers Union will take all steps open to it to prevent such uses of its material, its name, or the name of *Consumer Reports.*

For Linda, Mike, and Eric

CONTENTS

SECTION IV: IMPROVEMENTS

SECTION V: TAXES

SECTION VI: OTHER WAYS TO OWN A HOME

FOREWORD

Buying and owning a home still lies at the heart of the American Dream. Every year several million Americans embark on this great adventure. But for the first or even second-time home buyer, purchasing a house, condo, or co-op can be an alternately bewildering, intimidating, or tedious procedure requiring knowledge and understanding of many sorts—not to mention patience and a little luck. Some people find the various complexities and financial commitments of a real estate transaction so daunting that they stay put in a disadvantageous rental situation rather than actively pursue the many benefits that home ownership has to offer.

There are a number of books currently available on the subject of home buying, but many are geared to the real estate speculator or investor and focus on the supposed "instant" profits to be made by leveraging a real estate purchase. Others are general information books that often contain detailed and overly technical information and terminology.

How to Buy a House, Condo, or Co-op is intended to fill a pressing need in the home-buying literature for a basic primer for the average first-or second-time home buyer. Its language is easy to understand, its scope is comprehensive, and its aim is to provide the reader with all the essential information needed successfully to look for, negotiate, and close on a home. The book is divided into six sections: the buying process, the search for a mortgage, buying insurance, planning for home improvements, paying taxes, and finding alternate ways of owning a home.

We wish to stress, however, that the advice contained in this book is intended for educational purposes only. Because laws, customs, and practices may vary from state to state, readers are urged to seek appropriate professional advice with regard to any specific real estate transaction.

Some 54 million Americans currently own their own homes. Given the choice, most of us would elect to own our own home rather than rent. Since careful advance planning is the key to a successful home purchase, we hope that the information and advice in *How to Buy a House, Condo, or Co-op* will help the consumer to realize his or her dream of home ownership.

HOW TO BUY
A HOUSE, CONDO,
OR CO-OP

SECTION
I

THE
BUYING PROCESS

1

OWNING YOUR OWN HOME

Owning a home is part of the American Dream. We've been raised to believe in the value of home ownership, to think of it as something to strive for—and as the most momentous financial move we'll ever make.

It's no coincidence that as children one of our favorite pastimes is "playing house." From our first schooldays we learn that the desire to own a piece of land is an essentially American idea. We're plied with stories about plucky pioneers who carved homesteads out of the primeval forests and later the prairies and the deserts of the southwest. Thomas Jefferson even asserted that a nation of small landowners was essential to a flourishing democracy.

Evidently, this cultural conditioning has been successful. According to the National Association of Homeowners, there were 84 million homes in the United States at the beginning of 1985, 54 million of which were occupied by their owners.

Without a doubt, there is great personal satisfaction in owning one's own home. Home ownership represents a certain degree of financial success and personal accomplishment; it's a sign that you've "made it." The sense of security in owning your own shelter is nothing to be scoffed at, either. In fact, most home buying is largely motivated by these kinds of intangible benefits.

Then there are the tangible benefits such as tax deductions, growing property values, and fixed mortgage costs—all strong inducements toward home ownership.

While the rewards eventually may be substantial, the actual process of home buying can be long and arduous. Initially, the search for a suitable and affordable home can be exhausting and time consuming, and the process of negotiating the right price, mortgage loan terms, and the conditions of a contract can be full of pitfalls for the novice home buyer. Real estate agents and attorneys can be a big help in this regard, especially since home inspection procedures and the intricacies of the closing require a good deal of quickly acquired knowledge. The actual owning of a home is a long-term commitment with financing sometimes stretching as long as thirty years; maintenance and upkeep of a house and grounds is a constant expense in time and money. But most experienced homeowners will agree that it's all worth the trouble. Let's examine some of the principal advantages of owning your own home.

YOUR OWN SHELTER

Homeowners enjoy the sense of security that comes with owning and occupying their own home.

Owners of single-family dwellings are free to do what they like with that property, as long as they observe local zoning restrictions. They can add rooms, improve the landscaping, put in a swimming pool and play area in the yard, or attach a garage. They can choose the type of roof and windows they'll install, the color of interior and exterior paint, and the style and quality of carpets and drapes. Most importantly, single-family homeowners enjoy an unsurpassed degree of privacy.

For those benefits, homeowners assume higher expenses for maintenance and take on more risk than renters. The homeowner must be willing to stay in a home for at least a few years in order to profit from the move and thus must maintain financial stability and a long-term commitment to the community.

If you are among the one in four first-time home buyers who will choose to buy a condominium or co-op rather than a single-family house, you may not be able to alter that property to make drastic improvements. But then, you are also free from the burden of property upkeep and can still enjoy a level of security that is not available to renters. Because co-ops and condos most often are built in clusters or as large buildings, many people believe that this form of housing is too similar to renting to justify the investment. However, condos and co-ops today come in such a variety of settings that the market should be investigated before being ruled out.

A Sound Investment

Over a long period of time, few investments return as much as property. Real estate is cyclical, meaning that there are periods of several years in which housing prices remain stable or perhaps even drop in some areas. But over a 30-year period, owner-occupied housing has had an impressive track record. During the Great Depression, stock market values dropped nearly 90 percent; during the 1930s, property values dropped 34 percent. During the recession of the mid-1970s—the worst since 1929—housing values climbed 10 percent a year.

The National Association of Realtors reports that from 1966 to 1980, the median price of a family home climbed from $20,000 to nearly $70,000. Today it's much higher in most areas of the country, even with a cyclical tapering off of growth and a flattening of values.

The Association also reports that in 1985 the highest-priced houses in the United States were in California's Orange County, where the median house cost $135,200. San Francisco came in second, with average homes listing at $134,500. Boston held third place at $131,000; and fourth place went to the New York area, at $130,000. The lowest-priced homes were found in the frost belt, with the lowest average prices in the nation in Buffalo, New York, at $47,000.

In 1980, the National Association of Homebuilders asked consumers to name the best hedges against inflation. Three of every four Americans of whom this question was asked named single-family detached homes. In second place, named by more than half, were land investments. Eight percent mentioned condominiums, and 1 in 10 said that town houses were good hedges against inflation. The point is that even with the slowdown in growth following the meteoric price increases of the late 1970s, housing still tops the list.

Housing continues to rise in value when held for several decades because desirable locations are limited and because everyone needs shelter. Other factors affecting housing values include the economic health of an area, interest rates, and the public's opinion about housing as an investment. Housing obviously is not as hot as it was 10 years ago, and many believe that real estate investments will never be as lucrative again. But if past history is any indicator, housing will increase in value in the future—not as dramatically as in the past, but it will increase.

As in all markets, supply and demand are constantly changing conditions. Demand is high at one point in the cycle and, as a result, construction increases. This leads to overbuilding, and supply rises too far. Prices then level out or even drop for a while. This cycle tends to repeat itself every five to ten years, according to most real estate market analysts.

GROWTH IN EQUITY

Your net worth—the value of everything you own minus everything you owe—will increase over the years you occupy your home. This investment growth results from your accumulation of equity in the house. Each payment you make is divided between principal (which goes to equity) and interest. The growth is slow in the early years, when most of each payment goes to interest, but the longer you live in your home, the more rapidly the equity builds.

If you purchase a home for $100,000 and pay off an $80,000 mortgage loan over 30 years, your net worth will have increased by $80,000 minus inflation. Above and beyond that, you will also own the market value of your home. Thus, if its value increases, you may make a substantial profit when it comes time to sell it.

CONTROL OVER INTEREST EXPENSE

To a certain degree you have greater control when investing in a home than you do in most other types of investments. While you don't have the liquidity advantage of most stocks and bonds, a fixed-rate mortgage (one where the interest rate remains the same for the entire period) will stabilize your living costs.

Lenders today are financing a growing number of home purchases with adjustable-rate mortgages (ARMs). With these mortgages, the interest rate is adjusted every 6 to 12 months. You can still have a limited amount of control over your interest costs, as most ARM contracts include a "cap," or a ceiling on the interest rate level during the term of the loan.

This total or partial control over interest expenses can represent a tremendous benefit over a loan period as long as 30 years. If interest rates go up, you enjoy payments at a relatively low cost in terms of interest. If they go far below what you're paying, you can refinance your home and get a lower rate.

Refinancing does involve additional costs. It's not as simple as going to a lender and asking for a new loan. However, if you're sure you'll be in your home for several more years, and if interest rates have dropped three percentage points or more since you bought the house, the additional one-time cost of refinancing will probably be justified by an overall lower cost of interest.

Payments Go Down, Not Up

Homeowners often actually enjoy decreases in the real cost of housing. This is due to a combination of a fixed monthly expense (in the case of a fixed-rate mortgage) and the effect of inflation on your income. It is reasonable to assume that over time you will earn more money, but since your housing payments are fixed, the burden of your mortgage costs goes down with each raise you receive. Over a long period of time, the percentage of your total income going to house mortgage payments can become a minor factor in your overall living expenses.

The value of money changes too; what today seems like a large burden for mortgage payments may represent a more reasonable expense in the future, especially if inflationary trends continue or accelerate.

Improvements Add Value

The addition to your home of extra rooms or a remodeled kitchen or bath or the installation of a swimming pool or solar heating can add to your equity dollar for dollar.

The opportunity for homeowners to improve their investments with borrowed equity cannot be matched in any other type of investment. If you borrow $10,000 in the form of a second mortgage, backed by the built-up equity in your home, and spend it to make an improvement, most of the money is invested back into your home. Although you deplete present equity by the amount borrowed, you increase the value of the home and the opportunity of future profits. Once you've paid back the money you borrowed for the improvement, you have added to the equity in your house.

Increases in Equity

Monthly payments against a mortgage and home improvements are not the only ways in which your home increases in value. Equity also grows as market values increase. It is not unusual to see a home purchased many years ago for under $50,000 double in value to $100,000 on today's market. This means that you could owe $30,000 on your original mortgage but have up to $70,000 in equity—more than you paid for the house.

YEARLY TAX BENEFITS

For federal tax purposes, deductions are allowed for all interest paid on the mortgage loan you obtain for the purpose of purchasing your primary residence (the home you live in for most of the year). Many states allow this deduction as well. Most tax experts agree that it would be highly detrimental to the housing market in the United States if the interest deduction for home mortgages was disallowed, and politically unacceptable as well. Therefore, while Congress limited the deduction for most personal interest under the Tax Reform Act of 1986, it preserved the deduction for the interest paid on a mortgage for a primary or secondary home.

These tax benefits can make a substantial difference in the amount of tax you'll owe the government, and can actually reduce your housing costs. Many people who think they can't afford the move from rental payments to mortgage payments should look at the after-tax costs, which often are more financially advantageous than most renters think.

Since most of the mortgage payments you make during the first few years of home ownership go toward payment of the interest on the mortgage loan, your tax deduction for real estate can be sizeable. If your marginal tax rate (the rate at which you pay federal and state income taxes) is 30 percent, every deduction you can include will reduce your income tax liability by 30 cents on the dollar. Every $100 of interest costs you only $70, after the tax savings are taken into account.

To demonstrate this point, look at the total interest costs on a $70,000 loan (with a 30-year term) at 12 percent. In the first three years, your total interest expenses are:

Year 1	$8,386.33
Year 2	8,354.11
Year 3	8,317.81

But if your tax rate is 30 percent and you already itemize on your tax return, the true after-tax cost of interest is significantly lower:

Year 1	$5,870.43
Year 2	$5,847.88
Year 3	$5,822.47

To what extent home ownership is advantageous as compared with renting depends on your individual tax rate and the amount of your rental payments. Over several years, your interest advantage begins to diminish as a higher portion of your payment goes toward the principal. However, the rate of decline is so gradual that it shouldn't be part of your comparison ratios when you are first thinking of buying a home and comparing housing and rental costs.

For comparison purposes, assume that rent on an apartment or house averages $550 per month. With a 30-year, $70,000 mortgage, you're responsible for $720.03, or $170 more per month. The additional costs may appear to be too much of a burden at first glance, but if your tax rate is 25 percent or more, that's not the case. For example, at a tax rate of 25 percent, your house is $10 cheaper per month than paying $550 in rent after the tax benefits are figured into the comparison.

OTHER TAX BREAKS

DEFERRED GAINS. Unlike other assets that you sell at a profit, you are allowed to make a gain on your home and defer taxes until later. Under the new tax law, as before, as long as you purchase a new home that costs as much as or more than the home you sell within two years, there's no tax due until a later sale date.

Even if you buy a new home that costs less, you are taxed only on the difference between the selling price and the purchase cost. Thus, only a portion of the gain is taxed.

A ONE-TIME TAX BREAK. If you're age 55 or older, there is another benefit allowed under the tax rules. This is the once-in-a-lifetime exclusion from tax of as much as $125,000 in profit from a home sale.

This special benefit is designed for people who retire and subsequently sell their homes after many years of ownership. At that point in life, one's income most likely will be lower than it was during one's prime working years. This rule allows retired people to sell their homes without reinvesting and still retain most—frequently all—of their accumulated equity completely tax-free.

RISKS

There *are* risks in home ownership. One of the greatest is that you won't be able to afford to keep up your mortgage payments. Another is that the value of your property, for whatever economic or social reason, may decline.

These risks can be minimized by most home buyers. Most foreclosures result from one of two causes. Either the buyer purchased a home way beyond his or her financial capabilities, or financial reversals such as the loss of a high-paying job, disability, or the death of the family's wage earner were to blame. Job loss will jeopardize both owned and rented housing—it's one of the risks we all must live with, and it shouldn't prevent you from seeking to own your own home. Moreover, you can be insured against unexpected loss of income from death or disability. When you buy a home, it is essential to acquire the right amount of insurance protection so that the house will not be lost along with your earning power.

The new homeowner's other obligations include the necessity of maintaining the house and property for both personal and financial reasons, especially in order to retain its equity value. Every homeowner must face realistically the various expenses that automatically come with owning your own house. Even if you are a do-it-yourselfer by nature or necessity, there are many home repairs that will have to be done by outside sources—plumbers, electricians, roofers, tree surgeons. Maintenance expenses crop up frequently enough so that you must manage carefully in order to get the essential repairs done when needed and still maintain your monthly budget for living expenses.

Your life-style will change, of course, as you find more and more of your disposable income going toward the maintenance of the family home—the annual vacation may have to be sacrificed for a new roof, or the purchase of a new car put off in order to replace a gas burner before the heating season arrives. However, if you have had the home thoroughly inspected by a reliable professional home inspector prior to purchase, you should know what to expect in the way of immediate or upcoming major repair expenses.

There are, of course, other regular expenses involved with owning a home: real estate taxes, utility charges, water bills, sewer taxes, etc., plus the other outlays required to maintain a house and property, such as lawn equipment, extension ladders, and other tools—some of which may be costly. Ideally, these expenses should be built into your overall budget plan *before* you purchase your home.

In summary, if you protect yourself as much as possible against the risks that come with home buying, and plan ahead carefully, your housing investment is likely to be a gratifying and profitable one.

SUPPLY AND DEMAND

What's on the market, and what are people willing to pay for it? That is the essence of supply and demand. Many factors go into this constantly fluctuating balance, including the following.

INTEREST RATES. There have been instances in the past when rates were so high that it was nearly impossible for sellers to find buyers for their properties. In the late 1970s, for instance, mortgage interest rates approached 20 percent.

When this happened, the prices of houses became secondary. Financing terms dictated whether a property would sell, real estate agents became experts at locating competitive interest rates, and a number of so-called creative financing alternatives became the norm.

POPULATION. When the number of people looking for housing exceeds the number of housing units available, prices are pushed upward. To meet the demand other, more affordable kinds of housing are often created. The condominium market originally was an example of this phenomenon; buying a condo was seen as an affordable way to become an owner. Today, however, in many areas condos cost almost as much as single-family homes.

Population trends shift, just as interest rates do, resulting in changes in the supply and demand cycle. One reason for the tremendous demand for housing during the late 1970s was that the "baby boomers"—children born after World War II—were reaching ages 25 to 35, the prime home-buying years.

COST OF CONSTRUCTION. When construction materials are expensive and labor costs are high, home prices will be affected. Developers will adjust by building lower-quality houses or by raising prices (or both).

AVAILABILITY OF FINANCING. Just as changes in the interest rate have a direct effect on people's ability to buy homes, the amount of money available to lend to home buyers will affect the prices of these homes. The federal government and its programs play a significant role in this process through the Government National Mortgage Association, the Federal Home Loan Mortgage Corporation, and the Federal Housing Administration.

The policies of private lenders have an impact as well. If it is profitable for lenders to lend money through mortgages, they will do so. However, if it is more profitable to invest that money elsewhere, there will be less available for residential loans. Some lenders regulate the amount of mortgage lending they carry at any given time.

EMPLOYMENT OPPORTUNITIES. In any area, job prospects will have a significant impact on the housing market. The failure of a single dominating industry can be devastating to housing in that community; families will be forced to sell and move, and the number of foreclosures will increase as unemployment rises. A home buyer who is not affected by such an economic reversal may find some bargains; however, the downward spiral of property values in the community may limit the potential for selling that house at a gain somewhere down the road.

In areas where companies are growing and expanding, the opposite is true. New construction cannot keep up with the demand, and housing prices rise.

SUPPLY. Cycles change constantly. A supply reaction means that new construction will stop. A demand reaction means that new home construction will explode. But at some point the cycle will reverse, and the market then must adjust. To judge where a community is in the real estate cycle, look at the number of available houses and note whether it is increasing or decreasing.

Since houses are usually sound investments, you probably expect to make a profit by selling your home one day. But just as you need shelter today, you will need it as long as you live. You may make large profits from your real estate investments. However, chances are that most of that profit—and perhaps more—will have to be reinvested in your next house.

Rapid growth in property values, such as that seen in recent years, is unusual and shouldn't be expected to occur regularly or to the same degree in real estate markets throughout the country. You should consider your home a long-term investment and not expect to make a profit for the first few years.

2

ALTERNATIVES TO OWNING A HOUSE

The decision to buy a home should not be made lightly. Some home buyers have been tempted by books and seminars that promise untold riches in real estate and shamelessly promote complex schemes to make anyone a millionaire, "no money down."

The reality is this: Real estate is a solid investment that requires a commitment—personal as well as financial—on your part. It could be the largest transaction you'll make in your entire life. A down payment is only the beginning; ownership involves ongoing mortgage and tax payments and expenses for maintenance and improvements. Also, real estate doesn't mysteriously appreciate in value. It depends on both upkeep and a continuing market demand.

In short, make sure you're ready.

If you buy before you're financially able, it will probably be a decision you'll sorely regret. You may be forced to sell the house at a loss or, worse, default on a loan you can't afford, lose your down payment, and ruin your credit rating. If this occurs, gaining approval on a loan in the future will be much more difficult, even when you are financially solvent and prepared to buy.

Put off buying a home if any of the following applies to you:

1. Your income is too low; you can't afford mortgage payments that are substantially higher than rent.

2. You're not sure that you want to remain in a particular community; you may want to try another area within the next five years.

3. Your job does not permit you to stay in one area, or your

employer may transfer you to another location at frequent intervals.

4. Financial freedom is a high priority; you're not willing to tie up the money required for a down payment or pay more for a house than you would for rent.

However, you are ready to invest in real estate if you have a solid, steady income (especially if your marginal tax rate is high enough that you'll benefit from the mortgage interest deduction), if you know you will stay in your community for several years, if you don't expect to be transferred to another job soon or are willing to refuse a transfer, and if you recognize the responsibility involved in buying a home and are willing and able to commit not only to a down payment but also to the monthly payments on a mortgage loan.

RISK

Both the decision to buy and the decision to delay involve risks. The risk of waiting is less immediate but just as important. If you're ready but delay making your move, interest rates may rise, making your mortgage payment substantially higher when you finally buy. On a $75,000 loan for 30 years, the difference between 12 percent and 13 percent is $58 a month. That may not seem like much, but multiply it over 30 years and the difference is more than $20,000.

The prices of homes can rise. In some markets, they can skyrocket. Between 1972 and 1973, for example, home values in some parts of the country—notably the west—nearly doubled. At the same time, interest rates went up.

Meanwhile, for every year you delay, you'll be doing without the tax advantages of home ownership. There's also the risk that the demand for rental property in your area will grow and your rent will increase substantially.

BEING A RENTER

For some people, there are advantages to renting.

Rents have not increased at quite the same rate as the cost of buying a house. Part of the reason for this is the large number of people who prefer home ownership. Another reason is the fact that renters move more frequently than homeowners; as most seek the same or lower rents, they temper the demand for rental housing, thus maintaining a certain level in the cost of renting. In the 10 years ending in 1980, 9 of every 10 renters moved, while fewer than 6 of every 10 homeowners changed address. In addition, some communities have rent controls that prohibit the rise in rental costs from exceeding a fixed percentage or amount per year.

Part of the cost of owning a home is the high cost of maintenance and utilities. Usually, renters have far less expense in inside or outside upkeep.

In an apartment, utility costs are usually lower because supplying heat and light to a complex of 10 or 20 apartment units is less expensive per unit than paying for the same utilities in a three-bedroom home.

But renting has notable disadvantages. The greatest disadvantage is that rents do rise, sometimes precipitously. Not enough new apartments are being built to meet the demand. The result is a tight market, with many areas showing low vacancy rates and a high demand. Home costs, in comparison, may be higher at first but are fixed (with a fixed-rate mortgage) for as long, in some cases, as 30 years.

Along with this, there is the uncertainty of how long a period of time you may rent your shelter. The owner of your building may sell to someone else, resulting in higher rents, or the units may be converted to co-ops or condominiums, often forcing you to buy your unit or vacate it so that someone else can buy it. This conversion phenomenon is on the rise in some areas.

Typically, this occurs when a new owner buys a building and cannot afford to make the necessary changes to increase the value of his or her investment; income from rents simply isn't enough to fund those improvements that would increase the property values. Instead, the units are sold one at a time, enabling the owner-investor to make a profit without financing any of the major improvements needed.

As an apartment renter, you live very close to your neighbor. This makes renting a life-style that offers less privacy and imposes the obligation on you to be more considerate of your neighbors than would be necessary in your own house. Even worse, you may be subjected to noisy and inconsiderate neighbors who make your life unbearable.

In your own home, the quality of your living quarters is largely dependent on how well you maintain the property. In an apartment, you must depend on the owner and manager for the maintenance and repair of your immediate surroundings. Many apartments are in older buildings that have not been kept up over the years, and the owners often are unwilling to invest more money to satisfy tenant requests for improvements or repairs.

The decision to buy or rent also depends on where you plan to live. For a city dweller, renting may be less expensive than buying, even when the tax advantages of home ownership are taken into account. Urban apartment dwellers don't necessarily have to own a car, don't pay for commuting, and don't have to deal with the constant maintenance and upkeep of a house.

RENTING WITH AN OPTION TO BUY

Renters who want to buy a home but lack cash for a down payment may be able to purchase a home on an option basis. This arrangement became more common in those years when both interest rates and the prices of many homes were prohibitively high and many sellers found it to be the only practical way to find a buyer. The most common option arrangement is one in which the prospective home buyer becomes a tenant and pays rent plus an extra amount of money that is to be applied to purchasing the home at a later date.

In one case, for example, a house was rented for $400 a month and the tenant made payments of $600. The additional $200 was applied toward a down payment. Within 30 months, $6,000 was accumulated, representing 10 percent of the proposed sale price of $60,000. The owner agreed to help with financing by granting an additional 10 percent loan to the buyer. The balance—80 percent of the market price—was financed by a traditional lender.

The amount of the deposit required with a rental with option to buy varies with the amount of rent, the asking price of the home, and the amount of time allowed for the accumulation of a down payment.

For many people, such an arrangement, which also is called a lease option, is the most practical way to buy a home and sometimes the only way. The trade-off is that you may pay more for a home or for rent in the interim than would be required otherwise.

It is wise to enter a lease option contract only if the price of the home has been agreed on in advance. This is the most common arrangement. Without such an agreement, you have in effect no assurance that you'll ever have enough for a down payment.

The contract should clearly spell out all conditions, including when the option date will arrive, how option money will be handled (will it be deposited in a separate interest-bearing account?), what will happen to the extra amount you have paid if you decide not to buy the house, and so on. If you decide not to exercise your option, you may lose a portion of the money you put up in order to reimburse the seller for not being able to sell the property as planned. However, most of the deposit should be returned to you immediately.

In some contracts, return of this money is contingent on the seller's subsequent successful sale of the property. This means that if the seller enters a new lease option agreement, your money can be tied up for years. Insist that the contract spell out exactly *when* your money will be refunded.

3

THE QUESTION OF AFFORDABILITY

What can I afford? is the most basic and most pressing question for most first-time home buyers. Obviously, if you cannot afford a down payment and monthly payments, nothing else matters. Unfortunately, in many areas housing prices have risen so steeply, down payments are so large, and mortgage payments are so costly, that home ownership seems beyond the reach of anyone who hasn't already built up equity in a home.

Don't give up, however. You can put yourself on a realistic budget and save money for a down payment. You can resign yourself to accepting less of a home than the capacious Tudor of your dreams, at least as a first house. Educate yourself and approach the housing market as an informed buyer.

Begin planning before you even think of looking at any houses.

1. Set a standard for what you can afford to buy, based on your current gross income. You may decide that you cannot buy a house that costs more than two and one-half times your annual gross income. For example:

Annual Income	Maximum Price
$20,000	$50,000
30,000	75,000
40,000	100,000
50,000	125,000

2. Be willing to settle for less in your first home. Setting too high standards, demanding everything from parquet floors to a Jacuzzi, undoubtedly will put you in too high a price range.

You may find some real bargains in so-called fixer-uppers or handyman's specials—homes that have been allowed to deteriorate and need a lot of work. These can be as much as 20 to 40 percent cheaper than other well-maintained houses on the same block. If you're the handy type, you can do much of the work yourself, bringing the house up to market value quickly and making your investment grow much more rapidly than the perfect house next door. Be prepared to spend time and money fixing up the place. If you can't do the work yourself, be prepared to hire professionals and to pay them accordingly.

3. Decide how much you can afford to put down on a house. Should you put down as little as possible? Some people think so. Or do you want to invest 20 percent or more? It depends on how much you have saved and what the effect will be on your monthly mortgage loan payments.

4. If you don't have much money saved, start a savings plan now for your future down payment and stick to it. In a number of years even relatively modest savings can grow substantially. For example, saving $2,000 per year for five years ($10,000) grows to $13,192 at 9 percent interest, or to $14,513 at 12 percent.

If you want to get a competitive rate of return and at the same time ensure the safety of your savings, avoid speculative investments that may suddenly decline in value. Many personal money managers suggest investing in money market funds, treasury securities, and time deposits.

Avoid the three most common mistakes many families make when they attempt to save money:

1. Saving only what's left over from a paycheck after basic expenses have been paid. Instead, make your savings contribution every month a "basic" expense, to be regularly paid, just as you pay your monthly bills. And invest it first, before paying any other bills.

2. Setting an unrealistic budget. Don't expect to save a larger portion of your income than you actually can afford. Unexpected expenses are inevitable, so allow some room for them in your budget. You won't stick with a savings plan if it isn't practical.

3. Misusing credit. Avoid overusing credit or bank loans. If you commit yourself to regular monthly payments on a debt for several years, it will be that much harder to save for a down payment on a house.

If you decide that you are ready to buy, plan to look for houses in the off season. Avoid the spring and early summer "jump," when most people look for homes and sellers may have the advantage.

TAX CONSIDERATIONS

There are other things to weigh when you evaluate the prospect of becoming the owner of your own home.

The "real" cost—that is, the cost after deductions on your federal tax return have been taken into account—should be used when comparing the cost of your current shelter with that of a new home. After-tax payments are not as high as they appear at first; in fact, they may be closer to what you pay in rent than you think.

You must keep two things in mind when computing real cost, however. While your deductions will be significant in the first few years, the deduction for interest will decline every year. It is a slight decline: In a 12 percent mortgage with a 30-year term, less than 7 percent of the loan is paid off after the tenth year. This means that if your original balance was $80,000, you will still owe nearly $74,000, but your total payments amount to $98,000. The rest—more than the total amount of your loan—will have gone toward interest. This ratio between principal and interest diminishes over time and eventually interest is reduced to a small portion of your total monthly mortgage payment. However, that happens only in the last 8 or 9 years of those three decades, when more than half the total payment finally goes toward payments on the principal of the loan.

Most tax experts now believe that, for political reasons, Congress will continue to preserve the deduction for the interest you pay on your mortgage loan on your primary residence. In the most sweeping tax legislation in 40 years, the Tax Reform Act of 1986, Congress phased out the deduction for consumer interest paid on personal loans, credit card debt, auto loans, and other similar loans. However, Congress left virtually untouched the interest deduction for mortgages on primary residences (and secondary homes). Of course, by reducing the marginal tax rates on incomes, Congress did lower the overall benefit of the mortgage interest deduction for homeowners.

Furthermore, the Tax Reform Act of 1986 does sharply restrict taxpayers' use of real estate investments as tax shelters.

DEFINING "AFFORDABLE"

As your income rises over the years, the cost of housing becomes less burdensome, since mortgage costs are fixed (with a fixed-rate mortgage) or controlled (limited by rate ceilings in most ARM contracts). In other words, with time, housing is not only a sound investment with a growing value but one that should become less of a financial burden as well.

The growing equity in a home is another matter to consider. It represents a tax-free source of money that can be borrowed on for improvements (that further increase the value of the home) or other investments, or can be used as a larger down payment on a more expensive home in the future.

With all the financial, tax, and income questions to be considered, the term "affordable" clearly will mean different things to different people.

If you have a large amount of money for a down payment, you certainly can afford to look at a wider range of homes than will be the case if you have little or nothing. But you should also keep in mind that you still must qualify for a mortgage loan.

Even with a 20 percent down payment (the usual amount required), you may not qualify for financing on the house you like. In addition, all the closing costs involved in buying a home can add up to hundreds of dollars, perhaps several thousand.

There are no bargains to be had in the lending market, so beware of "creative" financing. What sounds like a good deal today only delays the day of reckoning later when you must pay for what you have bought—leading all too often to financial troubles and perhaps eventually to the loss of your home. Be very thorough in your research on offers that include extremely low initial interest or interest-only payments.

One alternative you may want to consider is leasing with an option to buy (see chapter 2).

When buying a first home, you need to strike a balance between affordability today and marketability later. You can afford only so much, so why invest in a home that's larger than you need right now? On the other hand, a home with a good location and floor plan will be more marketable when and if you decide to sell and will be more likely to appreciate in value. In other words, look at homes not only with a buyer's but with a future seller's eye.

One way to strike this balance is to think in terms of what your family's minimum requirements for living space will be for the next five years. Planning beyond that isn't practical, since needs change as a result of unforeseen circumstances. Moreover, if your primary concern now is being able to afford a home, there's no point in thinking in terms of a lifelong permanent address.

What are your family requirements at this time and for the next few years? What features will make your home easy or difficult to sell in five years' time, if you should decide to move?

SOME BUYING CONSIDERATIONS

LOCATION. This is one of the most important considerations when planning to purchase a home. Houses may be updated, renovated, and improved but neighborhoods, areas, and communities tend to retain their basic character and market values over long periods of time. Is the neighborhood of your choice a safe and pleasant place to live and perhaps raise a family? Is it readily accessible to schools, transportation, and shopping? Look for an area where homes sell quickly and easily (ask your real estate broker or banker for this information). It's a good sign if the average house stays on the market for three months or less; if it is usually six months or more (and the house is not wildly overpriced), look elsewhere.

Avoid neighborhoods with large numbers of poorly maintained homes, too many "for sale" signs, or a residential area encroached on by commercial outlets.

APPEARANCE. To be a good investment, a house should be fairly conservative in design. An unusual shape to the windows or slant to the roof, odd-shaped rooms, or a poor layout all detract from the appeal of a house to a future buyer. A good investment home also fits in well with other homes in the immediate area.

LIVING SPACE. Look for a home that is planned for the occupants' comfort and convenience. This means that the floor plan is laid out intelligently with an easy flow from one room to the next. It means that the house is not overly expensive to heat or cool. (High ceilings or large windows facing the daytime sun will raise utility costs.)

EXPANSION POTENTIAL. Can a room easily be added on? Is the yard large enough so that a first-floor addition can be built without violating the local building code? Or could you add on a second floor without making major changes in the foundation or radically altering the appearance of the house?

ROOM SIZE. Are the rooms, especially the kitchen and bathroom, a comfortable size? Buyers can be turned off by a small, poorly equipped kitchen or a bathroom with similar deficiencies. Basic features—such as three bedrooms and two bathrooms—always make a house more marketable. Even if you don't *need* those features, it may be wise to invest in them now in order to be able to sell at a fair profit later.

4

WORKING WITH
AN AGENT

In order to buy a home, you must find suitable houses that are currently on the market at a price you can afford. You can locate available properties through word of mouth, local newspaper listings, or sometimes just by "for sale" signs in your neighborhood of choice. Ultimately, though, most buyers find houses through local real estate agents.

THE REAL ESTATE AGENT

To understand the relationship between the real estate professional, the seller, and the buyer, you must first understand what the term "agency" means.

Whenever one person is given the authority to act on behalf of another, there is an agency relationship. The *agent* is given these rights by the *principal* (usually the seller) in the transaction.

A real estate *broker* matches sellers and buyers in a real estate transaction. When a homeowner wants to sell, the broker is retained to act as agent for the seller. In this relationship, the seller is the principal.

In other words, the broker-agent is working for the seller, not the buyer.

A broker can employ a number of other people to carry out transactions between sellers and buyers. The real estate *salesperson*, for example, represents the broker, who represents the seller.

The terms "broker" and "agent" in real estate are confusing because there are two levels of agency involved: the agency existing between a seller (in most cases) and the brokerage firm, and the agency relationship between a broker and his or her employees, the salespeople.

Keep in mind that the buyer is almost always a customer and is not directly part of the agency relationship. However, an agent can, in a sense, work for the buyer by showing homes that are in the right price range and that have all the features the buyer seeks.

A professional holding the title "Realtor" (a registered mark) is a member of a local real estate board that has an affiliation with the National Association of Realtors (NAR). He or she subscribes to NAR's code of ethics and has completed a course of study to earn the designation.

Salespeople who work for realtors can earn the title Realtor-Associate, having been qualified and licensed by the local board or by the NAR itself.

A "Realtist" is a member of the National Association of Real Estate Brokers, another trade organization that sets professional standards and has a code of ethics for its members.

WHAT TO LOOK OUT FOR

Shop around for a real estate broker. There are about 2 million brokers in the United States, with about 600,000 holding membership in the National Association of Realtors. The full-time professional, who is more likely to be experienced and to get the best listings, is more likely than not a member of this organization.

Ask friends and relatives for referrals to certain real estate agents. Bankers and loan officers of local savings and loan associations are another excellent source for referrals, as they work regularly with real estate agents in appraisals, property purchases and sales, and financing. Call the local real estate board and ask for the names of the highest achievers in the area (commonly the "realtor of the year"). If you have worked previously with a national franchise real estate company and were pleased, ask for referrals to affiliated agents in your area. A real estate attorney, accountant, financial planner, or other professional you trust also can refer you to a reputable real estate agent.

Agents can show you homes listed through their brokerage or with someone else since most brokers use a Multiple Listing Service, which means the commission will be split between the listing agent and the selling agent. The exception to this is the so-called exclusive listing. If you want to see a particular property and it is listed with one agency only, you must work through that agency. In that case, you will have no opportunity to interview the agent and decide whether he or she is a person you can trust and work with.

Look for the following caution signs when dealing with an agent:

1. You are consistently shown homes *above* your maximum price range even after you have clearly told the agent what you can afford. In all fairness, if you have set your sights far below the realistic market price for the type of home you seek, the agent has no choice. But if you know there are homes available in the price range you specify, an agent should show them to you. When the agent doesn't, it can mean that that particular agent simply doesn't have listings in your price range or that the agent hopes eventually to sell you a more expensive home than you intend to buy.

2. You indicate a preference in area, size of a home, or type of property but are shown homes that don't meet these specifications. This may mean that the agent shows those particular homes to everyone. Again, it may indicate a limited availability either in the local market generally or for that particular agent.

3. The agent overly "confides" in you, stating that the seller is "anxious to sell" or letting you in on other inside information. This is most likely a sales ploy the agent uses all the time. Keep in mind the agent is a deal-maker and his or her chief aim is to get the buyer and seller together.

4. The agent tries to tell *you* what you want, regardless of what you say. This is irritating as well as unprofessional. A good agent is one who respects your needs and makes an effort to match you with suitable houses in the area of your choice.

5. The agent offers you tax or legal advice. The agent is not a lawyer, only someone who is licensed to bring buyers and sellers together. Agents offering such advice are in over their heads.

6. The agent argues with you about an offer you want to make on a house. It is the agent's responsibility to communicate all offers to the seller even if it eventually means a lower commission for him or her on the deal. If an agent thinks your offer is unreasonably low, he or she will tell you so. But if you're determined to place your offer, insist that the agent follow through.

You have the right to work with any agent you want. If you're unhappy or uneasy with his or her selling technique or lack of results, switch to someone else. You're under no obligation to work with one agent, even if that agent has spent a lot of time showing you homes. Of course, if you find a broker or salesperson whom you feel you can trust and who seems tuned in to your needs, by all means use that agent exclusively. Since most homes today are multiple listings, your agent should be able to show you almost any property available, regardless of the original listing agent (although there may be a period of a week or two when the original listing agent has the property exclusively to show to his or her customers).

A word of caution: if you see a property with one agent, and a few weeks later see that same property with another agent, you are obligated to credit the first agent with the commission if you decide to purchase that property. You are liable to a lawsuit if you ignore the first agent's right to the sale.

You can hire an agent—a buyer's broker—to act on your behalf. This is common practice in commercial real estate and involves payment of a finder's fee for a particular property. This is not necessarily a smart move for the consumer seeking a residential property. Such an agent may be induced to work a little harder for you, but the fundamental relationship between agent and seller will not be affected—you still will take a secondary role as long as someone else is paying the agent's commission.

NEGOTIATING THROUGH AN AGENT

When you make an offer through an agent that is lower than the asking price for a home, wait until the seller responds before telling the agent that you're willing to pay more. If you confide in the agent that you will in fact pay a higher price, you can be sure that the agent will let the seller know. Keep some distance. Recognize that the agent will be compensated by the seller, not by you.

The agent *can* be a valuable go-between. If you are negotiating directly with the seller, it is easy to reach an impasse. But an experienced agent can bring both of you to a mutually acceptable price and ultimately to an agreement.

It isn't unusual for offers and counteroffers to go back and forth, often going beyond the price of the home alone. Matters of financing, the itemization of fixtures to be included with the sale of the home, the date when the seller will vacate the property, payment of inspection and closing costs, and the amount of money that will be paid to fix a deficiency in the house can all be included in the negotiation.

BUYING WITHOUT AN AGENT

Should you look at a home being sold directly by an owner, without an agent's involvement? Some people think they will save money by doing so, since the owner does not have to pay a real estate agent's commission and can price the house accordingly. Others are afraid to buy a home in this manner, fearing that some step in the buying process may be illegal or incorrect or that certain deficiencies in the house may be covered up until it is too late.

You may find some bargains working with a FISBO (for sale by owner), as real estate professionals call them. But always protect yourself by hiring the expertise of an attorney, an appraiser, and an independent home inspector before you decide to buy.

In addition, look for a conscientious homeowner who has taken the time to prepare for prospective buyers. The owner should have a fact sheet on the home, listing its particular features without exaggeration, as well as the age of the house, heating costs, taxes, possible assumable financing available, and the asking price. This responsible approach by the owner will help to convince you that he or she is serious about selling and is not just "testing the market."

Many people who have tried to sell their own homes lose potential buyers because they are overly anxious, too aggressive, or too inflexible on the price and terms of the sale or, conversely, fail to mention certain features of their home that may appeal strongly to the buyer. Ask the seller if he or she is willing to have the contract and its terms reviewed by your attorney. If the seller isn't agreeable to this, look elsewhere. Once you have decided that you're seriously interested in a home, you'll want an appraisal and inspection done—at your expense. There's no reason why a seller should object to any of this. If the seller does, beware. You expect direct and complete answers to your questions from a real estate agent who represents the seller; you expect the same treatment from the owner selling directly. No one knows the answers better.

In any case, never be bullied into an agreement. Always take the time to consider the property carefully, with comparable properties in mind, and make a sensible offer according to your evaluation of a fair price for the house and your needs and financial restrictions.

5

HOW TO EVALUATE AREAS

Americans may talk a blue streak about their roots, but statistics show that our society is one of the most mobile in history. Families outgrow houses, career changes often dictate one move after another, and moving up to a more luxurious home is a basic part of the American Dream. In short, the search for optimum housing is one of our national obsessions.

The average first-time buyer in this country stays in the same home for less than five years. But no matter how often the move, the criterion for a new home remains the same: location, location, location. This old saw of the real estate industry is still true—one sees it reflected in the much higher prices paid for homes on desirable streets and located in the more prestigious areas of a town.

If you're looking for a home and already have a particular area in mind, you have a good starting point and can concentrate on the five basic criteria for choosing one community over another:

1. Tax base
2. Quality of public school system
3. Services: garbage collection, sewers, police, fire protection, etc.
4. Accessibility to the workplace
5. Available recreation facilities

TAX BASE. The important question is where the tax dollars of a community come from and what you get for your tax dollar. In many towns property tax is the chief source of funds, and so the tax rate will be higher than it is in a town that has a high proportion of business and industry that helps offset the cost of service for its residents. Do some research on your own and check out the tax situation, including any recent assessments, the needs of the school system, zoning changes affecting real estate development, the condition of town buildings and equipment, and any recent cutbacks in services and recreation facilities.

SCHOOLS. This factor is of prime importance to any home buyer, whether married or single, with or without children. The quality and condition of the public school system will affect your tax rate and certainly the future desirability of your home to any potential buyer. Find out class sizes, ratio of teachers to pupils, special programs offered, and the number of courses offered at the high school level. Check out how the students rate on standardized national tests and how many go on to college. We strongly recommend that parents visit the school personally, attend classes, and ask lots of questions.

SERVICES. Most well-established communities provide all or most of the basic services: garbage pickup, water and sewers, social and library services, fire and police protection. But some don't and residents must pay for private garbage collection and other services. Check to see whether this is the case in your town, and whether the roads are regularly plowed in winter, what the extent of police protection is, and if the local fire department is staffed with volunteer or full-time, paid employees.

ACCESSIBILITY. Few people want more than a one-hour commute to get to work, although in today's climate of high-priced suburban housing many are forced to go far beyond it. Good access to the workplace determines property value, and communities in close proximity to where the jobs are rank high in desirability and price. Proximity to commuter railroads, buses, and highways is an obvious necessity.

RECREATION. This factor influences some buyers, but not all. Parents with small children or teenagers are especially sensitive to the availability of local recreation facilities—ball fields, parks, playgrounds, pools, indoor municipal facilities.

The serious buyer should also check the statistics on home sales in the area during the past year. Find out the asking and selling prices of a number of homes.

Check the "swing" between the asking prices—the prices the owners originally wanted for their homes—and the actual selling prices. (A local real estate agent or banker will have these figures.) Compare sales for the entire year and compute the difference. As a rule, a stable and hence desirable neighborhood should show a swing of 5 percent or less.

If the swing is greater than 5 percent, it means one of three things: Houses were overpriced to begin with; there weren't enough interested buyers to pay those kinds of prices; or the market is in flux.

The swing test can also point to faults in homes built by one developer that make for very low resale values. Recurrent flooding, mud slides, or other problems in the area can also result in resale difficulties.

Next, check on how many homes sold over a period of time. This helps tell you whether the neighborhood has become more or less attractive to house seekers. If it seems that a large number of homes are for sale at one time, find out why.

A second telling statistic is the time it takes to sell the average home. (Again, local real estate agents and bankers have these facts.) In a very desirable neighborhood, homes will sell in three months or less. In the average area, selling time takes between three and six months. Steer clear of any area where the average home takes six months or more to sell.

New construction has its good and bad aspects. It can indicate a healthy growth and a rise in property values as more families move to the area. It also can mean more shops, better schools, transportation facilities, and other conveniences. However, new construction can bring congestion, noise, and heavy traffic patterns that may not be to your advantage as a homeowner.

SOURCES OF INFORMATION

The following people and associations can be of invaluable assistance in your investigations of the housing market.

REAL ESTATE AGENTS. Ask a number of agents which areas of the city or town are the best maintained. Keep in mind that many agents will emphasize those areas in which they have a large number of listings and that their interest is in selling properties and earning commissions. Don't necessarily expect to find the most objective information here.

REALTY BOARDS. A county board is more objective than an individual local real estate agent, and can point you toward an area where owners take pride in their homes, houses sell easily, and property values remain high.

HOMEBUILDERS' ASSOCIATIONS. Check the state or local association to find out which areas have seen the most dramatic growth. Where are the new developments and which areas of the town have well-constructed older homes?

REMODELING CONTRACTORS. Check with several local contractors to find out which neighborhoods are being generally improved and updated by the residents. A well-kept area is bound to be one where homeowners are adding to the value of their homes and, in turn, to the value of the entire area.

INSURANCE AGENTS. A local professional who sells a lot of homeowner's insurance can tell you easily which neighborhoods regularly increase in value and where homeowners regularly update their insurance policies in order to protect their real estate investment.

BANKER OR LENDER. Bankers are in constant touch with real estate agents and appraisers, and can tell you where the fewest foreclosures occur, where values rise consistently, and where the best risks are, from their point of view.

PLANNING DEPARTMENT. The local planning department of the town can tell you whether an area is on a floodplain, for example, and whether there has been recent flooding, mud slides, or other natural disasters.

THE FIRE DEPARTMENT. Check on the number of fires in the community you're considering, as compared with the average in the general area. A high incidence of fires in the vicinity, especially those thought to involve arson, is a sure sign that a town is in trouble.

THE POLICE DEPARTMENT. Be sure to ask for statistics on crime. Is serious crime on the rise, or is it falling? How does the area compare with adjacent communities?

A LOCAL NEWSPAPER. Check back issues at the local library to get some idea of the problems of an area. If there are major unresolved issues affecting the value of homes, be sure that you understand all the ramifications.

THE NEIGHBORS. Perhaps the most important source of information is the people living in the area you're considering. If they respond to your general questions about the neighborhood with enthusiasm, that's a good sign. Listen for positive statements about the climate, traffic, noise, quality of schools, transportation and shops; all are strong indicators of the quality of the community.

A NEIGHBORHOOD CHECKLIST

Any complete evaluation of a neighborhood should include the following:

TRANSPORTATION. Access to commuter railroads, buses, and highways should be convenient.

TRAFFIC. Increasing traffic means growth in the area. Too much, and the quality of life will suffer. If there is heavy traffic close to the home you're considering, think about the possible noise and pollution level and the effect it will have on your life-style.

PRIVACY. Ideally, homes should be placed on a street so that residents may expect peace and quiet in their own homes and yards.

PARKING. Besides adequate personal parking availability close to your own home, you will want ample parking space for your guests. A lack of parking space for visitors can become a major inconvenience.

SHOPPING.
Large shopping centers should be within reasonable driving distance. There should be some local shopping facilities closer to your home.

CHURCHES. Be sure that the neighborhood is not far from the church or synagogue of your choice.

SCHOOLS. The quality of schools in the area is of paramount importance, especially if you have children. The schools should be easy to get to, and transportation for your young children should be provided by the school district.

HAZARDS. Check to make certain there are no potentially dangerous hazards nearby, such as quarries, polluted streams, or toxic waste dumps. Also inquire about the possibility of radon contamination in the area.

NOISE LEVEL. Check during peak traffic hours and throughout most of the day. Any nearby industry, airport, train access, or other source of noise can be highly disruptive, especially in the summer months.

POLICE PROTECTION. Make sure police regularly patrol the neighborhood, respond promptly to calls, and in general adequately protect the homeowners in the area.

FIRE SERVICES. Find out how far the closest fire station is and the response time to a call. Ask about the number of fires in the neighborhood, and find out where the nearest fire hydrant is relative to your prospective home.

TOWN PLANNING. The best neighborhoods are well planned, with conveniently arranged streets and a buffer zone between the residential and commercial areas.

NEIGHBORS. The mix of residents in the area should ideally complement your family. If you have children, make sure there are a number of families with children of similar ages, so that your children will not be isolated.

CULTURAL OUTLETS. How accessible are museums, libraries, and/or concert halls? Are there active neighborhood clubs and groups promoting different varieties of social and cultural contact?

RECREATIONAL OUTLETS. Note the number of parks, restaurants, theaters, and other facilities in the area.

HOSPITALS. Determine the distance to the closest hospital and find out how many other hospitals there are in the area. Make sure that local physicians and hospitals accept your form of health coverage and that a paramedic or other emergency unit is stationed nearby.

CLIMATE. If the area is oppressively hot or cold for part of the year, be sure you and your family can tolerate such extremes in temperature.

CRIME LEVEL. Is violent crime on the rise, or is it declining? Inquire about recent break-ins and robberies in the neighborhood by checking the local police statistics, newspaper reports, or with the neighbors.

TERRAIN. If many homes are located on hills or directly below potential slide areas, that's a danger signal. Find out whether there has been any flooding in recent years and whether the neighborhood is on a federally designated floodplain.

UTILITIES. Taste the tap water and check the local water facility for recent reports on the quality of the water supply. Find out whether refuse is collected promptly and whether the neighborhood is satisfied with the local utility service.

NEIGHBORHOOD IMPROVEMENTS. If the local government is improving its buildings, parks, and other facilities, that's a very positive sign.

ZONING AND ASSESSMENTS. Zoning rules should be strictly enforced. Make sure that residential areas are kept free of commercial activity. Find out from the local municipal offices, if possible, whether any special assessments are planned for the neighborhood and determine what the cost will be to each homeowner. Your county planner can supply a zoning map and a description of each zoning classification. With this information in hand, check the neighborhood you're considering to see whether there are any obvious violations or questionable uses of property.

6

HOW TO EVALUATE HOMES

If you're anything like the average home buyer, you'll look at so many houses that your head will begin to swim. In fact, you should look at a number of homes in order to have a means of comparison and an understanding of what your particular budget can buy. You also should go about your search systematically, completing a checklist and sketching a floor plan for those homes you are seriously considering. This will help later, when the details and differences of these homes become a blur and you start confusing the pantry of one house with the back porch of another.

You can begin your evaluation of each property by breaking it down into three broad categories:

1. Convenience and taste. You must like the house. This means that it must suit your individual taste. It's in the right area, giving you most of the conveniences that are important to you. Its floor plan and overall style are generally what you have in mind, and you think that you can live there with the degree of comfort you want and expect.

2. Structural integrity. The smart home buyer knows how to inspect certain aspects of a house both inside and out and he or she comes equipped with a complete list of points to check. But the same buyer also knows that some types of home inspections are best left to the experts (see Chapter 8).

3. Investment potential. As an investor, you want to find a home that will increase in value over the years. Its location, style, and floor plan must appeal to future occupants.

EXPLAINING YOUR PREFERENCES TO THE AGENT

You'll most probably look at homes in the company of a real estate agent. Before leaving his or her office, be sure both you and the agent have a clear understanding of exactly what you're looking for.

AREA. By narrowing down the area, you also narrow down the number of homes to be viewed. Going through homes is an exhausting and sometimes discouraging process, especially if you're not looking in promising neighborhoods to begin with. Apply the tests listed in chapter 5 before setting foot in a single house. It will make your search and the agent's job a lot easier.

HOME STYLE. If you understand the difference between a Cape Cod and a Carpenter Gothic, you're a step ahead of the game. However, you needn't be an architectural historian to be able to communicate with the agent about the type of place you're interested in viewing.

Emphasize that you want to steer clear of any homes with poor design features, such as an odd exterior appearance and proportions, or a house constructed of shabby building materials.

SIZE. Most home buyers describe the house they seek in terms of the number of bedrooms they need, but there is more to consider.

First, try to anticipate your needs for the next 5 to 10 years. Assume either that you will be able to move up to a larger home if your family is growing or that you will be able to add on improvements. You might, for example, tell the agent that you are looking for a home to which another bedroom can be added easily or for one with a room that can be converted to a bedroom at a later date.

You should also be specific about the size of the living room, kitchen, and bathroom. For some, a garage will be an important feature, whether for parking, storage, or conversion to another use at a later date. Perhaps the size of bedrooms is important; anyone used to large bedrooms may have a difficult time accepting the extremely small ones found in many lower-priced tract homes, for example.

If you've looked at many homes and have paid attention to total usable size, you can specify the square footage you need in a two- or three-bedroom house.

PRICE. This is the most common guideline. It should not, however, be the only preference you express to a real estate agent. If it is, you will be subject to a hit-or-miss approach to home buying. An agent can't possibly know what to show you in terms of area, style, or size unless he or she knows more about your needs and taste.

When you look for homes by reading ads in the local paper, price is usually the main thing you have to go on. This is bound to cause a lot of frustration. If you want a home in a particular community, and the majority of homes there are above your price range, you will certainly be attracted to one that is priced much lower than the rest.

After viewing several such lower priced homes, however, you will come to see:

1. They're generally the most run-down houses on the market.

2. They're in the poorest areas of town.

3. There are likely to be problems such as flooding or an inconvenient location.

4. The floor plan is poor.

5. The ad sounded good, but the house didn't live up to its promise.

Putting such "come-on" ads in the paper is one of the most effective ways for real estate agents to attract new customers. Once you respond and are shown all these substandard properties, the agent will probably tell you, "If you could look at homes priced a little higher, I could show you some really nice ones."

At this point you may see some better homes, but you are still looking for a house passively. You are allowing an agent to show you what's available without specifying what *you* are looking for.

Take more control of the situation and go to an agent with a list of your preferences, including:

1. The areas of town you prefer

2. A precise house style: age, design, even a specific floor plan

3. Size, including the sizes of rooms or lots

4. Price

If you are told there's absolutely nothing on the market at your price that will give you everything you seek, check with another agent before you decide to lower your standards.

USING DIAGRAMS

Plan to diagram the rooms of the homes you are seriously considering. A simple sketch will suffice. It doesn't have to be something an interior decorator would be proud of, just a basic summary of the floor plan. But include any special features in each house, such as split levels, fireplaces, or walk-in closets.

Use grid paper for accuracy, estimating the size of each room and trying to keep as much as possible to scale. One grid square can represent one foot or more, depending on the type of paper you use. In most cases, a real estate agent will be able to tell you the measurements of each room, making your job much easier.

We show two diagrams on page 40. Note the features of each house that make one acceptable and not the other:

Good features (first plan):

1. Privacy: those inside the house are not in view of the front entrance
2. Good use of space
3. As few corners as possible
4. Good overall shape and "flow" of rooms

Bad features (second plan):

1. No privacy: people in the kitchen, dining room, or living room are in full view of the front entrance
2. Much wasted space
3. Garbled floor plan with too many corners
4. Odd overall shape of living space

On a diagram, you can also jot down your quick impressions of a house as you go through it. You will spend 20 minutes or less in each house if you're typical, maybe more if you're seriously impressed.

In houses that are top prospects, take more time with the diagram, noting the locations of all windows, doors, and closets. Make notes about the type of flooring, the quality of the walls and ceilings, and any appliances that come with the house. Write comments about the exterior as well. Comment on the landscaping, how much maintenance will be required, the appearance of the roof, how recent the paint job appears to be, the size of the yard and the total lot, and your general overall impression of the place.

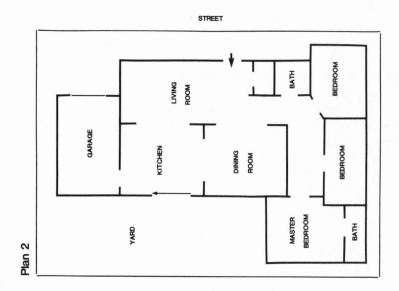

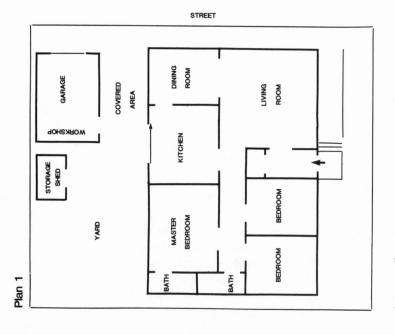

home diagrams

WHAT SELLS A HOUSE

There are certain conventional features of a house that most home buyers are looking for and usually put at the top of their list. They include:

HOUSE APPEARANCE AND STYLE. Does the house conform in general with the size, style, and period of the other homes on the block? Individuality is one thing; distinct unconventionality is another. In general, for good investment potential and high resale value, the house should fit into its neighborhood, area, and climate.

CONSTRUCTION MATERIALS. Wood siding is the most commonly used material, although in warmer areas it is also more susceptible to termite damage. Brick, stone, and granite are more uncommon but highly desirable, while stucco is an attractive and generally acceptable building material although it is subject to cracking in frigid weather. Vinyl or aluminum siding is practical and relatively maintenance-free.

LANDSCAPING, VIEWS, AND SITING. There is no doubt that a view substantially increases the value of a home. The prospect of daily glimpses of a river, hills, or far expanses is tempting to any home buyer. But how absolutely necessary is that view, and is it worth the often inflated price of such a property? That's your decision, of course. But be aware that, although the view may pall eventually, you keep on paying for it for a long time to come.

An expanse of lawn is another factor to consider. A large piece of property, especially if it consists of manicured lawns and shrubs, needs almost constant care and maintenance except perhaps in the dead of winter. In order to maintain the value of the property, you'll have to do it yourself or spend quite a bit of money for professional help. If you like gardening, fine. If you don't like the idea of constant maintenance, choose a house with a minimum of lawn upkeep, perhaps with self-maintaining plantings and/or trees.

The actual siting or placement of a house becomes an important comfort feature once you have lived in it year round. How many rooms face south and get the rays of the late morning or early afternoon sun? Do many rooms face north, with little or no direct sunlight? Is there too much shade from overhanging branches of trees or tall shrubbery? These considerations will affect your heating or electric bill, if not the resale value of the house.

Privacy is something else to think about. Some screening trees or plantings can make a big difference. If you feel there is inadequate privacy from the street or from a neighbor, yet the house itself is promising, consider the possibility of erecting an attractive fence or planting fast-growing shrubbery to achieve a screening effect.

GARAGES. Every buyer expects to get a garage with a house, preferably two-car, with plenty of storage. But this convenience is not always available, especially in older homes. You may have to settle for a one-car garage, and perhaps a shed in the back of the house for bicycles, lawn mower, and other gardening equipment. Garages located under the house are unpopular because of the dangerous proximity of automobile fumes and possible heat loss to the rooms above. Detached garages are not particularly desirable, especially in colder regions, while carports are acceptable only in warmer climates.

DRIVEWAYS. A steep incline or decline to the garage can affect the resale value of a house, especially in the colder areas of the country, where snow and ice can create a drainage problem and a driving hazard. In general, a blacktop or concrete driveway is the most sought after by the buyer. Gravel driveways can be muddy in wet weather, dusty in summer heat, and generally messy the year round.

TERRACES, DECKS, PORCHES, AND PATIOS. Every homeowner wants an outdoor area for warm weather relaxing, outdoor games, and perhaps barbecuing. Backyard flagstone or concrete patios or terraces are probably the most convenient areas for such recreational activities, with decks and porches a close second depending on the style of the house. Roofed and screened porches are always popular.

WINDOWS. In colder climates, combination storm and screen windows are an appreciated addition to any home. Self-insulating windows are a plus feature and are usually found in newer homes.

ENTRANCEWAYS. First impressions are always important. An attractive front entryway and an adequate foyer increases the saleability of any house. However, the back door probably will be used more often than the front door by most homeowners, so a mud room or back hall where coats and boots can be stored is a wonderful convenience for families. If the laundry room is close by, that's even better.

TRAFFIC PATTERNS. A convenient "flow" of living space in a home is vital to the routine of daily living. Survey your prospective home and ask yourself: how many rooms have to be walked through to get to another room? Is the bedroom area sufficiently separated from other living areas? Is the family room close to the kitchen? Is there more than one way to get to the kitchen and to the stairs? Is the downstairs lavatory conveniently placed for family and guests? All of these considerations will affect your life-style in the years to come.

KITCHENS. The kitchen is certainly the most significant room in the home for most families, and one of the most important factors in the resale value of a house. An eat-in kitchen with plenty of counterspace and adequate cabinets is the most desirable and sought after by home buyers. Modern, up-to-date appliances are necessary adjuncts of a good kitchen, along with a good supply of natural light, adequate storage space for brooms, ironing boards, etc., and if possible, laundry facilities. A pantry would be a plus. Remember that a kitchen is expensive to renovate and update, and a pleasant, roomy, and convenient kitchen is an important element in the price of a home.

BATHROOMS. As with a kitchen, a modern, up-to-date bathroom is a prime consideration for a home buyer. A master bathroom plus a hall bathroom increases the value of a house quite dramatically, while a downstairs lavatory is usually a necessity, especially if there are children in the family. Check the tiles for cracking and loose grout and test the water pressure. Are there shower facilities? Is the ventilation good, with adequate window venting or a fan? Any sign of water damage in the ceiling below?

LIVING ROOM. A large living room is a popular feature in a home, especially if there is no family room. Ideally, the living room should be somewhat apart from the noisier, more active rooms in the home and should allow for some privacy. A fireplace is usually appreciated if not always used; there are some people who won't buy a home without one. It is advisable to have the flue and chimney checked out by a professional before using.

DINING ROOM. A formal dining room is a big plus, especially for people who plan to entertain a great deal. However, a dining area off the kitchen can be adequate and dining "L's" are common in condominiums and co-ops. Most buyers accept them if they are of an adequate size and in a convenient location. Dining rooms and areas should be close to the kitchen, with access also through the living room or foyer.

FAMILY ROOM. Home buyers, especially those with children, appreciate family rooms on the first floor. They take the pressure off the living room and can serve as the entertainment center for the entire family. Basement family rooms are outdated and generally disliked, although certainly acceptable if finished off and with good access to the outside.

LAUNDRY ROOM. A separate laundry room on the first floor is a real luxury and increases the resale value of a house. Second to that, a washer and dryer in the kitchen is acceptable to most home buyers. Basement laundry facilities are less popular, if only because it means trudging up and down stairs with baskets of laundry. Some new condominiums and houses feature upstairs laundry facilities near the bedroom areas, which delight many people and disconcert a few. In any case, the washer and dryer should be in good working order, with adequate shelving or clothes racks nearby.

CLOSETS. Is it possible to have too much closet space? A walk-in closet in the master bedroom is a big plus, as is a linen closet, foyer coat closet, broom closet in the kitchen, and a back door closet for boots and wraps.

ATTICS. The big, old-fashioned attic for family treasures is found only in big, old-fashioned houses. It's nice to have some storage space at the top of the house, but no one likes inconvenient ways of getting there. Pull-down stairs are acceptable for most people, but hard-to-get-to openings in closets and hallways are not.

BASEMENTS. Home buyers want an adequate, dry basement, if only for utilities and storage. Good lighting and access to outdoors is also desirable. Newer houses, especially in warmer climates, probably will have utility rooms somewhere off the garage or in the back of the house.

The basement, containing the foundation and the heating, electrical and plumbing systems, is the core of any house. The serious home buyer should carry a flashlight and look carefully for obvious signs of damage or deterioration in the basement and then hire a professional inspector to give the area a thorough review. Some possible damage to look for:

1. Termite damage—it's difficult to determine if a home is adequately protected against the ravages of termites. Rather, you should look for signs of termite infestation: tell-tale mud tunnels or evidences of swarming. The tunnels are the transportation system of the subterreanean termite, used by the insect to travel back and forth to the soil; "swarming" is the mating flight of the termites, when they shed their wings. Dried wings on sills and the basement floor are definite signs of a termite invasion. We strongly recommend that the home buyer hire a termite inspection service to perform a thorough inspection of the property and that such an inspection be a term in the purchase contract. (See Chapter 8 for further information on termites.)

2. Signs of water damage—look for water stains along the bottom of the basement walls. If it is apparent that there has been water damage, find out why and when, or hire a professional engineer to examine the basement area. Some water problems are solvable, others are not. In some cases, a sump pump will help. You may notice white "fuzz" on the walls of the basement or garage. This is called *efflorescence* and is caused by moisture and acids in the concrete. A little efflorescence is not serious, but a large amount calls for more investigation, since it is a sign of chronic moisture and dampness.

3. Settling—every new house "settles" a bit eventually, and you may find hairline cracks in most basement foundation walls. But large cracks in the foundation, doors and windows that bind and show signs of cracks, may indicate uneven settling and merit further checking by a professional inspector.

A BASIC CHECKLIST

The prospective homeowner, flashlight and checklist in hand, will also want to take a look at:

WALLS AND CEILINGS. Check for cracks and holes, especially in plaster walls and ceilings. Seams in wallboard should be invisible and smooth. Be alert to any signs of water damage, such as stains, peeling, etc.

FLOORS. Hardwood floors are highly valued and need periodic care. What condition is the floor under the carpets? If you can look underneath, fine. If it's wall-to-wall carpeting, you'll probably have to take the owner's word for it that the floors are in good condition. (It's a good idea to have that contingency put into the contract.) The floors in the rest of the house should be level and solid.

ATTIC. If it's accessible, check for water leaks and any signs of rodent infestation. The leaks will show as dark stains on the wood of the rafters, especially around the chimney or vent areas. Droppings and shredded nesting materials in corners is a sure sign of infestation by squirrels, bats, or mice. Make sure there is adequate ventilation—vents in the roof will allow excess heat and moisture to escape. Of course, check for the amount and type of insulation between the roof rafters or floor joists of the attic.

ROOF. The most common roofing material used in this country is asphalt shingles, which usually last for about 15 to 20 years. If it is quite apparent to you that there are bare spots on the shingles or the shingles look suspiciously worn and curling at the edges—then the house probably will need a new roof in the near future. (Have an inspector take a closer look.) Check the gutters and downspouts as well—most today are made of aluminum or plastic and are relatively maintenance-free. If the gutters are made of wood, check them carefully for signs of rotting.

ELECTRICAL SYSTEM. You'll need a professional inspector or electrician to thoroughly review the electrical system in a house, but you can spot a few things yourself, such as: does the house carry 220-volt wiring, enough to run air conditioners, electric ranges, other appliances? Check the circuit breakers (usually found in the basement area) or the main electricity board for this information. (The agent and/or owner can also furnish this data.) Look also for adequate outlets in all the rooms—there should be at least one for every 12 feet of wall.

HEATING SYSTEM. Gas and oil furnaces are the most common type of heating systems found in American homes. One is supposed to be safer than the other, or cleaner, or cheaper to run. But your chief concern is the overall efficiency of the unit in the house you are considering—how much does it cost to heat in the coldest months of the year? An inspector can check out the efficiency of the unit and the owners should furnish you with the bills of the previous years so you can see exactly how much it cost them to heat the house. Of course, some people prefer a warmer house than others, so you should take this into consideration. Take a look at the thermostat—is it up-to-date? Automatic?

HOT WATER HEATER. Again, a job for an inspector to check out thoroughly. But see if the hot water heater is a circulating system attached to the furnace (no storage capacity and you must keep the furnace on all summer, even if only to heat the hot water) or a free-standing hot water system (an 80-gallon tank will ensure sufficient hot water for a family of four). An electric unit is usually more expensive to run than gas. How old is the unit? If it is more than 12 years old, it may have to be replaced in the near future.

PLUMBING. Again, difficult for most home buyers to appraise on sight. Unless the house is brand-new, about the only thing you can safely judge is whether the piping is brass, copper, galvanized iron, or PVC plastic. Unless there are obvious signs of leakage, rely on a professional inspector to evaluate the actual condition of the plumbing system.

WATER SUPPLY/WASTE DISPOSAL. If you are thinking of buying a house with its own well water, be sure to have the water tested before you do. Check the supply—is it adequate throughout the year? If the house of your choice has a cesspool or septic tank system for waste disposal, have a professional inspector review the entire system. How often does the tank or cesspool have to be cleaned out? Make sure you know the exact location of the tank, and get the name and phone number of the company that regularly services the system.

In summary, the average home buyer rarely has the time or the expertise to thoroughly review every facet of a house, especially the heating, electrical, and plumbing systems. By all means, check out the more obvious aspects. But ultimately you must rely on professional help for a complete, in-depth inspection of your prospective home. Problems that appear on inspection, unless of a very serious nature, should not deter you from buying the house as long as the owners are willing to either make the necessary repairs or lower the price of the house.

7

MAKING AN OFFER

A seller places a house, condominium, or co-op on the market hoping to attract viable offers. The asking price is usually a guideline—a general indication of what would be acceptable to the seller.

When a buyer makes an offer to the seller that is accepted, a contract is then created. To be valid and enforceable, the contract must contain the following four elements:

1. It must be in writing. Verbal contracts will not do in real estate transactions.

2. It must include an offer and an acceptance. There must be mutual consent between the two people entering the contract: in real estate, the buyer and the seller.

3. It must be within the law. A contract that violates the law is an invalid contract. For example, by law, both people entering the contract must meet certain requirements in regard to age and mental competence.

4. There must be a consideration. Something of value must be exchanged. The buyer offers to pay a certain price for a house, and the seller in return agrees to transfer title.

If at any time during negotiations for a house, condo, or co-op, you are not sure whether you are committing yourself to a contract, *find out before you sign anything.* Without careful and thorough examination of what you're signing, you may end up in a contract when you thought you were only testing the waters. If, even after checking every aspect of a deal, you are unsure about the commitment you are making, consult an attorney.

In the case of condominiums, this includes the terms of the offering plan and the Declaration of Condominium, as well as the by-laws of the association. If you are purchasing a co-operative apartment, carefully check (and have your attorney review) the offering plan, the by-laws, the latest financial statement of the corporation, and the proprietary lease. Of course, there are often numerous offers and counteroffers made between buyer and seller before an actual agreement on price is finally reached. Your best offer, even when not initially accepted by the seller, can be accompanied by a binder, or earnest money check, which will demonstrate your good faith in going through with the deal. All of these offers, by the way, should be in writing, for your protection.

If your offer is accepted, a contract is then drawn up between the buyer and the seller, and certain conditions, or contingencies, are specified (in the contract) that must be met before the contract is valid and binding.

Every contract should provide for three major contingencies: house inspection, termite inspection, and the buyer's ability to get a mortgage loan for the property. This is discussed in more detail later in this chapter and in the chapter on contracts.

THE COMPETITION

Home buyers always worry that they will find the perfect house, condo, or co-op only to lose it to another buyer with a better offer.

If you feel you absolutely can't live without that particular residence, you can do any of the following:

1. Make an offer at or close to the asking price. This will demonstrate your serious interest to the seller.

2. Do not attach any contingencies to the offer. Contingencies can include sale of a previous residence, obtaining financing, inspections, and repairs the seller must perform. However, this can be very risky, and legal advice is suggested before you attempt to do this.

3. Offer a deposit that demonstrates serious interest. You don't have to offer what the real estate agent says is the minimum deposit, which is common practice. Depending on your degree of interest, your deposit can be quite substantial.

4. Offer to pay part of the seller's closing costs or the cost of termite treatment, etc.

Remember, however, that if you do any of these things, you lose negotiating leverage. If your desire for the house is so blatant, the seller will be less willing to negotiate. He or she will know you are eager to buy and may even make a counteroffer that includes more demands than you're willing to go along with.

Successful negotiation—offer, counteroffer, and acceptance—involves a delicate balance. Ideally, you want to express your sincerity without giving up everything before the discussions have barely begun.

BUYER'S AND SELLER'S MARKETS

Competition for a particular property depends to an extent on its desirability. It may be a home of historic importance. It may be a particularly good buy or have an ideal location in a highly valued community. Obviously the more desirable property will attract greater interest among buyers.

These and other factors of supply and demand will determine whether you will find yourself in a buyer's market or a seller's market.

Ideally, you want to buy—and later sell—in perfect market conditions. Many homeowners have done this with proper timing and some luck. You may not be so lucky. Because of market conditions beyond your control, you may find yourself in a seller's market, where bargains are few and far between.

Making an offer in either market should begin with the complete neighborhood and house inspections covered previously in this book. An informed buyer who thoroughly understands a particular area and the important qualities of a house will always do better than one who has not bothered.

Even in a buyer's market there are potential pitfalls as well as opportunities. The opportunities are:

1. There are more sellers than buyers. Take your time and look for the best possible house for your money.
2. Lenders will be eager for business and are more likely to offer you competitive rates.

Make sure, however, that you understand why it's a buyer's market. Will the economic factors that contribute to the current housing situation affect you and the future market value of the house? For example, there can be hidden flaws common to all the houses built in that particular area or development. These can be due to such things as poor construction, a recurring problem with flooding, or a rapid increase in crime in the neighborhood.

In a buyer's market, with so many homes to choose from, you may be less apt to do all the necessary preliminary research. After all, you may figure that you can dictate terms to eager sellers and lenders, so why bother? If you decide that research isn't important because there are bargains everywhere, you're asking for trouble. No real estate investment is risk-free, and you should always know, to the best of your ability, what you're getting into.

In a seller's market, the rules are the same but the approach is different. Here the pressure is on you. Sellers are the ones dictating terms. Beware: There are problem houses even in a seller's market, and these may be pushed the hardest. Make an offer with the competition in mind and with an eye on the economic conditions ruling the marketplace, but here too, follow the rules of common sense. Know the market before you jump in.

These points should be kept in mind in a seller's market:

1. Don't be rushed into a decision you're not sure of, even if it means passing up what might be the perfect property for you.

2. Be thorough in looking for mortgage financing. Since lenders in the area probably will be offering mortgages at higher rates, shop around for the best possible terms.

Be sure you understand why this is a seller's market. Are these current factors likely to change in the near future? If so, it may be wise to wait until they do. Again, don't let preoccupation with the competition cut short your necessary investigations of the area and of the house itself. If you do your preliminary homework, you'll be way ahead of the competition and better able to spot the better deals that may come your way.

CONTINGENCY OFFERS

Even if you've thoroughly researched the area, the house, and the supply and demand factors that are at work, your offer isn't necessarily going to be a simple purchase and sale agreement. There may be contingencies you will want to attach to the offer.

A contingency is a qualification you make in the contract. In other words, you offer to abide by the contract only *if* some other action or event takes place.

There are two forms of contingencies: those within the seller's control and those beyond it. A contingency that requires the seller to perform certain tasks is common in real estate transactions. The seller may be required to make needed repairs or pay for termite treatment, for example. Or your offer is made contingent upon the results of a professional house inspection. If the inspection turns up problems, the buyer can expand the contingency by requiring that certain work be done to correct them, or the buyer can re-negotiate the offer.

For both buyers and sellers, one of the most difficult contingencies arises when one's previous house must be sold. "Contingent upon the sale of an existing house" means that you make an offer, but the offer takes effect only after you sell the house you now live in. So many otherwise solid deals have collapsed because of the delays in unrelated transactions that many real estate experts suggest that you first sell your previous home before negotiating for another.

Outside the seller's control is the standard contingency of most contracts: that the buyer qualify for mortgage financing. For first-time buyers, this is an especially advisable contingency, as it provides a way out of the contract if a bank will not lend you sufficient funds to purchase the house.

THE OFFER

There are no standard methods or formulas for making offers—the state of the local real estate market, the location and general desirability of the property, and how much you really want it—will dictate the form and timing of your offer. It's wise, though, to ask a few questions about the sales profile of the house you have in mind before making an offer, such as the length of time it's been on the market, whether there have been any price reductions or previous offers, and if the asking price of the property compares favorably or not with the selling prices of other comparable houses in the area.

In a "hot" market, when housing is at a premium, your offer probably will be verbal and conveyed by your broker to the seller by his or her real estate broker. If you need guidelines, certainly you can't go wrong with a first offer that is 10 percent below what you honestly think the house is worth, regardless of the seller's asking price. If the seller counters your opening bid, your second offer should not be your absolute top price, but it should approach the true market value of the property as compared with other similar properties in the area that have sold recently. If the seller responds to your second bid with another counter you may be close to negotiating a price that will be satisfactory to both parties. However, many negotiations bog down at this point, and it is just here that a good real estate broker can make the difference and bring both sides together.

Of course, you may have considerably more leverage if the housing market in the area is "soft," if the seller needs to sell quickly, or if the house, for whatever reason, is not particularly appealing to most buyers. In that case, you can take more time and, after your first or second bid and with or without a counteroffer from the seller, leave the bid "in" with the broker and wait for the seller to respond. It's a good idea to accompany this offer with a binder and an earnest money check which will emphasize to the seller that you are seriously interested in the property.

In any case, make sure that any binder form you sign is subject to a contract to be drawn up later and signed by all parties to the transaction. Never make out your check to the seller directly. If you are dealing directly with owners, without an intermediary real estate broker, make the check out to their lawyer or yours, who will act as escrow agent.

Procedures vary over the country but usually, once your offer is accepted, you will be required to turn over to the broker a check for 1 percent of the total selling price of the home, as a sign of good will and intent on your part. Later, at the contract signing, this check will be returned to you, and you will give the escrow agent a deposit check for 10 percent of the total selling price. This deposit check will be held by the escrow agent in a special account until the closing.

8

OUTSIDE SERVICES

What happens if you make an accepted offer on a house, hand over a large down payment, and go to closing, only to discover later that there is a serious defect in the property? It may cost thousands of dollars to fix and your budget is already strained. Fortunately, there are a number of steps you can take *before you buy* that will prevent this disaster from happening. Some safeguards are required by law: For example, in some areas of the country termite inspections are mandatory. The prudent home buyer will take even more precautions.

There are many types of inspections that can be done on a piece of property. If a home you like is built on a steep slope, for example, and you're concerned about possible mud slides, order a soils test from a civil engineer who specializes in this kind of work. For a fee of a few hundred dollars, the engineer can tell you about the potential dangers of any sliding or erosion and put your mind at rest.

DIAGNOSTIC SERVICES

Today most buyers hire general home contractors or inspection services to check over a house before purchase as added insurance against the possibility of severe structural defects not visible at first sight. This is one of the most important contingencies of the contract. Diagnostic services are becoming more common also because real estate agents are increasingly being held accountable for defects that are discovered after the sale of a house. In the near future, home inspections, diagnostic evaluations, and contractor's reports doubtlessly will become as standard throughout the country as termite inspections are today.

Today only Texas requires a state license for home inspectors. This means that in most states anyone can hang out a shingle and offer to perform home diagnostic services.

However, there is a trade group, the American Society of Home Inspectors (ASHI), 655 15th St., N.W., Suite 320, Washington, DC 20005, that sets rigid standards for home inspection services. ASHI currently has 500 members located in most states. Members of ASHI must have performed no fewer than 1,000 home inspections or must establish equivalent experience (holding a contracting or engineering license, for example). ASHI members also must complete continuing education programs to keep their membership in good standing. Those accepted for membership charge $100 to $300 for a home inspection, depending on the region and the amount of travel involved.

In addition, there are a number of regional associations of home inspectors, many of which support the same principles and apply the same rules and standards as ASHI.

A reputable home inspector, for instance, will never offer to perform needed repairs and never should refer you to a contractor to perform such repairs either.

The depth of an inspection will vary from one service to another, even among ASHI members. However, every inspection should include an evaluation of the following:

- Foundations
- Doors and windows
- Roofing
- Plumbing and electrical systems
- Heating and air conditioning
- Ceilings, walls, and floors
- Insulation
- Ventilation
- Septic tanks and wells

The inspection doesn't necessarily determine whether a house is in compliance with local building codes, nor is it a guarantee or warranty.

A written report will be part of the service, but it is a good idea for the buyer to be on hand when the inspection is conducted. You can learn a great deal about home maintenance, ask questions, and learn more about the extent of possible problems.

The inspector can provide other valuable information. He or she can point out signs of a damp basement, for example, even when there is no standing water visible. The inspector also can tell you what corrosion or other water damage you can expect in the future. What about a roof's strength, cracks in the foundation, or water pressure? The inspector can educate you about these kinds of issues as well.

Armed with such knowledge, you can negotiate an adjustment in the price or make a conditional offer contingent upon the seller's repairing a problem. Or you can ask for a reduction in price or ask that the seller share the cost of repairs.

In cases that have gone to court, buyers have sued both the seller and the real estate agent, often months or even years after the sale date. In fact, to protect against this, real estate agents are more frequently ordering a home inspection as a matter of routine *before* negotiations on a home begin.

GETTING A HOME WARRANTY

Another protection you can buy is a form of warranty.

One of the most popular is the Home Owner's Warranty (HOW) Program which is offered by builders of new homes. The warranty is included in the price of the new house, through the builder. HOW is currently available on approximately one of every four new houses built in the United States today.

The program covers any and all defects in workmanship and materials for the first year as well as flaws in plumbing, electrical, heating, cooling, and mechanical systems.

Warranty of workmanship and materials is dropped after the first year, although major structural defects are covered for 10 years. The warranty includes a deductible—homeowners will have to absorb the first $250 of repair costs during the first 2 years of the warranty if a builder fails to make repairs and a claim to HOW is made.

Some ASHI-member home inspectors offer a form of warranty underwritten by an insurer who is willing to trust the inspector's professional evaluation of a home. This program costs $200 to $500 in premiums. For older houses or those with notable problems, the warranty can be granted with exclusions or for a higher premium than would be offered for newer homes. A warranty for these older houses may be limited to three years, with some plans including a renewal option for an additional premium. The older the home, the more advisable a warranty, even if it is limited in terms of what it will include and how long it will remain in effect. Other plans are offered through franchised real estate brokerages.

Whether you believe that you need a warranty, in addition to a comprehensive home inspection, is a matter of individual choice. The older a house, the more advisable a warranty, even if it is limited in terms of what it will include and how long it will remain in effect. Buyers of new homes should especially take advantage of any available warranties. A 1981 Federal Trade Commission survey of 1800 owners of new homes found that 62 percent of them had repair problems that were not corrected by the builder. Buyers also need to be assured that disputes will be settled promptly and that repairs will be made even if a builder goes bankrupt.

THE TERMITE INSPECTION

One of the most chronic and serious causes of damage to a house is deterioration caused by infestation of pests, especially termites. The actual damage is not visible to the naked eye, at least not until it has become extensive. By that time, parts of the wood underpinnings of the house can crumble in your hands. Untreated and uncorrected, a termite infestation eventually can cause a house to fall apart.

Subterranean termites—the ground-nesting variety—are the most destructive. They are found in every state except Alaska and are especially common in the temperate regions, notably California, the eastern part of Texas, and all the southern states. The U.S. Department of Agriculture estimates that the cost of termite control runs at least $250 million a year.

A pest control inspection is required in many areas as part of the preparation for selling a house. The seller frequently pays for the inspection, but a wary buyer should hire a second inspector to make sure that all damage is fully disclosed. The inspector will look for damage by drywood termites, powder-post beetles, and carpenter ants as well as subterranean termites. The presence of termites can be detected in a number of ways. The insects can be identified by sight. They have unelbowed antennae (unlike ants, whose antennae bend) and a thick middle body (an ant's body thins in the middle), and the winged variety has two wings of approximately equal size (in winged ants, the forward wing is noticeably larger than the other wing).

Another sign of the presence of termites is a periodic swarming of winged insects from the ground itself or from the wooden parts of a house. This occurs as part of the insect's reproductive cycle. A large number of discarded wings near the house or on the floor near doors and windows is sure evidence of a well-established termite colony.

Once found, termites are not easy to eradicate. Simply destroying the reproductive queen of a colony won't destroy the pests, as there are secondary reproductive females in all termite colonies. But a reputable termite inspection service should have the latest pest control techniques that will remove all traces of this serious threat to your housing investment.

How can you be sure that you're getting an honest report from a termite inspection service? Since there have been isolated instances of fraudulent reports from some services, ask experienced friends, real estate agents, or the local Better Business Bureau for referrals. As further insurance, call the county or state consumer fraud agency in your area to make sure there are no complaints filed against the inspection service of your choice.

In summary, it is highly recommended that the prospective home buyer make a termite inspection a contingency of the contract and pay for the inspection himself. If there is evidence of termite-caused damage to the house, the owner should be willing to pay for a full termite extermination treatment. In any case, make sure all extermination work is completed before you close on the property.

NOTE: As of this writing, the EPA (Environmental Protection Agency) has cautiously approved, with some modifications, the continued use of the toxic chemical chlordane as a treatment for residential termite infestations. But you should be aware that this chemical is still controversial and proven cases of severe illness and neurological impairment have been caused by the careless application of this chemical. Discuss this important question with your pest control service and choose another type of chemical if you want to avoid any possible complications resulting from the accidental seepage of chlordane into the living areas of your home. If you decide to use chlordane, have the house tested for possible contamination *before* you move in.

THE DANGERS OF RADON

Many experts now recommend that home buyers have their prospective house tested for the presence of radon. Radon is a naturally occurring, odorless, radioactive, carcinogenic gas that can seep into houses and cause major health problems—indoor radon is now estimated to be the number one cause of lung cancer in nonsmokers. Radon contamination is now considered to be a potential health threat in parts of all 50 states, affecting some 10 percent of American residences.

If the home buyer wants to have his or her house inspected for radon, it can be made a contingency of the contract, along with the building and termite inspections. Fortunately, in most cases radon problems are easy—and relatively inexpensive—to solve, so the presence of radon is not usually a good reason to forgo the purchase of a house.

For further information about radon in your area, call your state or public health departments. Or a reputable home inspection service should be able to give you more information about the various methods of testing for radon contamination.

9

THE CONTRACT

The contract process is a complicated one, and you may need someone to help guide you through it. Because there is so much to remember and act on, many buyers prefer to work with an attorney who specializes in real estate transactions. If you anticipate hiring a lawyer, do so *before* signing a contract or, even better, have one in mind before you make an offer on a property. By working with legal counsel throughout the entire process, you not only will have the security of working with a knowledgeable expert who is on your side, but you will avoid giving up important rights when you make an offer or a deposit on your new home. If you have already entered into an agreement without counsel, a lawyer can only tell you where you've made your mistakes—sometimes very costly ones.

Remember, when shopping for a lawyer, that it pays to look around. Fees are not regulated, and they vary considerably from place to place.

Once the buyer and seller reach an agreement on price, a contract is drawn up, which lists the names of the buyers and sellers, the price of the property, the address of the property being sold, the date and place of closing, and the signatures of each person buying the property and each person who currently owns the property. A contract can include practically anything, but the following are the essential contingencies (certain provisions that must be fulfilled in order that the contract be truly binding) in most real estate contracts today.

HOME INSPECTION. All prospective buyers want to make sure that the property they are purchasing is in good condition, and that the plumbing, electrical and heating systems, and roof are all in good order and working properly. A complete home inspection by a professional inspector should be done as soon as possible after an accepted offer—in fact, the contract usually specifies that it be performed by a certain date. Hiring your own professional home inspector is strongly recommended. If there are repairs to be made, it's always better to negotiate with the seller on price and then hire your own people to do the necessary work. That way you can be assured that a good job will be done.

TERMITE INSPECTION. Termites are more of a problem in some parts of the country than in others—however, a termite inspection is highly recommended for all home buyers. If termites are present, you can negotiate with the seller to have them exterminated (usually at the seller's expense) and any damage repaired. Or you can void the contract.

MORTGAGE. You will have to borrow most of the money for the purchase of the property unless you have enough cash on hand to pay the full purchase price. Securing a mortgage loan is a lengthy, tedious process, but it is the most vital contingency of the contract. It's important that the term of the mortgage and the amount of money you plan to borrow is spelled out in the contract, or you may find yourself legally committed to a mortgage you can't afford, or lose your deposit if you default. This is unlikely, but it can happen. The mortgage contingency clause also should specify a cut-off date—that is, the length of time you have to get the mortgage commitment. If you don't get a loan within that time, the deal is off.

TITLE CONTINGENCY. There should be a clause in the contract stating that the title to the property is free and clear, with no liens (claims) against the property. A title company conducts a title search, which the buyer usually pays for, unless otherwise negotiated. Contingencies, contract provision, legal customs, etc., can and do vary from state to state and jurisdiction to jurisdiction. The advice of an attorney should be considered before signing any contracts, especially if there are any special contingencies to be met. The buyer should be aware that, if any of these major contingencies are not met, the contract is void and the prospective purchaser must get a refund of all his or her deposit monies.

There are usually other common, if less urgent, contingencies in a contract, such as: a listing of what is removable from the premises by the seller and what stays with the house; a clause that the house or apartment be properly maintained until the closing and left "broom-clean" for the new occupants; and perhaps a provision for a day-of-closing inspection of the premises by the soon-to-be new owner.

Often a buyer has to sell a current home in order to purchase a new one. The practice of including this sale as a contingency in the contract varies considerably over the country. In California, for instance, it is virtually automatic, while in the northeast, it is rare. Of course, market conditions also influence sellers' attitudes on this point—if interest rates are high, mortgages hard to get, and buyers few and far between, the seller may allow such a contingency to be written into the contract. In a climate of low interest rates, readily available mortgages, and willing buyers, that may well not be the case.

ESCROW

One of the more confusing aspects of the contract process is escrow. Escrow is the temporary holding of money (i.e., a deposit and/or documents) by a third party until all the contingencies of the contract are met. The escrow agent establishes a special trust—an escrow account—into which both buyer and seller deposit whatever funds are involved in the transaction. This third party can be an attorney, a lender, a title company, or any other person or institution that is not a party to the real estate contract itself. Real estate brokers, who earn a commission from the seller for their services, are not usually used as escrow agents.

When the contract is drawn up, the buyer and seller should clear up the matter of who is to hold the monies involved, and who is to receive the interest from the escrow account. (Today, escrow accounts usually are interest-bearing.) This question should be clarified in the contract to everyone's satisfaction.

THINGS TO REMEMBER

Before the closing date, make sure the following steps have been taken:

1. All necessary inspections have been completed, reports issued and reviewed, and necessary repairs either completed or provisions made for their payment by the seller.

2. The title company has determined that the title is free and clear. A title report has been issued, as well as a title insurance policy.

3. All mortgage contingencies have been met, and the lender has set the date, time, and place of closing.

4. You have made arrangements for homeowner's insurance to cover the new property, and it will be in effect by the time you take title to the house.

5. During the contract period you and the seller have agreed on the exact date when the house will be vacated, including all furniture and personal belongings. If there is an overlap and the seller wishes to stay in the house beyond the closing, or the buyer wants to move in before the closing, an agreement must be drawn up stating all the particulars, and setting an appropriate per diem rate that is agreeable to both parties. If you have hired an attorney, he or she should be consulted since there can be substantial risks involved in such a situation.

6. Make sure you know the exact closing costs and the number of certified checks required by the lender and/or the seller. Check to make sure that you have the requisite amount of money in your checking account necessary to meet all closing costs. (see Chapter 10—Closing Costs).

7. You have looked over the vacated property and checked to make sure everything is in order as stipulated in the contract.

At the closing, the closing agent sees that all pertinent documents are signed and that the change in ownership is officially recorded.

HOLDING TITLE

During the contract period, you will be asked how you want to hold title to your home. You have several choices, depending upon the state in which you live. Your attorney, lender, or real estate agent can give you more information, but the general categories are:

JOINT TENANCY. This is the most common and practical form of tenancy for married couples, in which two people share one title. Property is jointly owned. In the event of the death of the first spouse, 50 percent of the value of that property is included in the estate of the deceased spouse. It is possible under current law for one spouse to transfer property to the other tax-free, so that the surviving spouse actually ends up with a stepped-up basis (current market value of the home) in that one-half of the property.

TENANCY IN COMMON. This is an arrangement in which two people each own a portion of a house as owners in severalty. There are two important considerations to this form of ownership. First, a single property owned in this manner is an undivided interest, meaning you cannot identify specifically which portion of the house is owned by each tenant. Second, each tenant can sell his or her portion without the consent of the other. For example, an unmarried couple could buy a house as tenants in common and, a year later, one could sell his or her portion to someone else. (All states recognize this form of ownership, with special rules in effect for Louisiana.)

OWNERSHIP IN SEVERALTY. You can hold ownership to your house in one name only. This is possible in all states, and may be necessary if your spouse is a minor. Even though you register your home in this way, your spouse may also be required to sign many of the documents involved in the escrow and property transfer process. This is legal in every state (special rules apply in Louisiana.)

The form of ownership should be considered carefully before signing the contract and escrow documents, particularly by unmarried couples buying homes or by those residents in states that do not recognize joint tenancy. In those cases, legal advice may be necessary.

For married couples, joint tenancy makes a lot of sense because, upon the death of one spouse, there is no question of valuation or transfer. Title simply passes to the surviving spouse.

10

CLOSING COSTS

The purchase price of a home is not only the amount you have agreed to pay the seller. First-time home buyers should be aware that eventually they will be faced with a baffling array of fees for everything from title insurance to property taxes. These fees are called *closing costs* since they must be paid at the time the transaction is "closed," and the title to the property passes from the seller to the buyer.

Again, the process of closing can vary considerably from one part of the country to another. But the essential fact of closing remains the same: it is at the closing that all monies are exchanged, fees paid, and title to the home officially passed from one to another. In response to many complaints and much confusion among buyers and sellers, RESPA, The Real Estate Settlement Procedures Act, was passed in 1974. Under RESPA, the lender is required to provide you with a list of closing costs, as well as a list indicating exactly what documents and services must be presented or completed before the closing.

For tax purposes, you should know that some closing costs are tax deductible. Others are not and can be added to the total cost of the home. This final cost is the "adjusted basis," or the true total cost of your new home. This is important because when you sell your home you must use the adjusted basis as the means to compute and report a capital gain on your income tax return, if there is such a gain.

The following are closing costs you will probably pay as a home buyer although they may vary, depending on your location and methods of purchase.

LENDER FEES

POINTS. Also called the *loan discount fee,* a point is 1 percent of the amount you borrow. A lender may charge one or several points for granting you the mortgage loan. In a highly competitive market, points are minimal. When many buyers are looking for loans and money is in demand, they can add up.

Some lenders offer mortgage loans for no points in order to attract business. Others offer lower interest rates but add on several points, often three, four, or more. The balance between loan rates and terms and the number of points added to a mortgage should be figured into any comparison of different financing agreements. Under the 1986 Tax Reform Act, points are tax deductible on the purchase of a principal residence.

The cost of points can add up quickly:

MORTGAGE BALANCE

	$40,000	$50,000	$60,000	$70,000	$80,000
1 point	$400	$500	$600	$700	$800
2 points	800	1,000	1,200	1,400	1,600
3 points	1,200	1,500	1,800	2,100	2,400
4 points	1,600	2,000	2,400	2,800	3,200

APPRAISAL FEE. This is the cost to the lender of hiring an independent appraiser to determine the current market value of the home you are buying.

TRANSFER OR ASSUMPTION FEE. This fee is charged for processing work involved in the transfer of an existing mortgage loan from the seller to the buyer, if there is such an assumable mortgage.

LOAN ORIGINATION FEE. This fee covers mortgage processing costs and can be a separate charge equal to one percent of your mortgage balance. In some areas, this fee is paid at the time of the mortgage loan application and is not refundable.

MORTGAGE INSURANCE. The lender may require that you take out a mortgage insurance policy, or you may request such coverage on your own. A mortgage policy is a form of life insurance that decreases with the balance outstanding on your mortgage. It ensures that, in the event of your death, the mortgage will be paid in full. Default coverage is another form of mortgage insurance required by some lenders. This form of insurance protects the lender if you should be unable to keep up your monthly mortgage payments. It is usually included in your monthly mortgage payment and remains in force until your equity in the house is 20 percent of the total or more. Although the lender benefits from this form of insurance, you pay.

CREDIT REPORT FEE. This fee is paid to an outside agency by the lender for a detailed report of your credit rating. It is sometimes paid at the time of loan application and is not refundable.

SURVEY FEE. A survey showing the boundaries and exact location of your property is usually required by the lender.

FEES FOR TITLE SERVICES

TITLE SEARCH. Every mortgage, lien, and attachment on a piece of real estate is recorded in a local or county office as part of a permanent record. A title search is the process of examining the recordings on a property to make sure that there are no outstanding liens or claims against it before you buy. As the owner, you would be liable for any such claims. In some states, an attorney is paid for the title search; in others a title company does the job.

TITLE INSURANCE. This is an insurance policy that protects you if there is an outstanding lien against the property. It varies with the price you pay for your home and by the area of the country you live in. The premium is paid once and is guaranteed for as long as you own the house.

NOTARY FEE. This is a charge paid to a notary public to guarantee signatures on certain legal documents involved in the transaction.

RECORDING FEES. This fee pays for the recording of your transaction at the county recorder's office.

TRANSFER TAX. This tax is charged by the state or locality as a levy on the transfer of the property.

OTHER CLOSING COSTS

ATTORNEYS FEES. If you privately hired an attorney, you will be required to pay his or her fees at the closing, or shortly after. If necessary, you will also be required to pay for the services of the lender's attorney as well.

ESCROW FEES. In some areas, the escrow agent charges a fee for handling the transaction of funds.

BROKER'S COMMISSION. Always paid by the seller at the closing, unless the buyer has made a special agreement in the contract to pay a part or all of the commission.

HOMEOWNER'S INSURANCE. Although not generally considered a closing cost, the lender will require you to carry adequate insurance protecting your new home against fire, vandalism, other casualties, and liabilities.

Different lenders have different policies on closing costs. In addition, the fees of local and state tax authorities vary greatly in different parts of the country. One rule of thumb claims that closing costs for a home buyer will range between 3 and 10 percent of the total purchase price of the home.

In any case, be prepared to expect some closing costs that may not be mentioned here. If you don't understand them, ask your broker or attorney to explain them.

PRORATING EXPENSES

One of the more confusing aspects of closing costs to many new homeowners is the prorating, or adjusting, of expenses. The day you take title to your new house rarely corresponds exactly with the paid-up dates of expenses such as utilities, fuel, taxes, and interest payments on the house and property. The buyer will owe the seller for any period after the closing that has already been paid for by the seller.

The actual calculation can be done in one of three ways, depending on the nature of the expense:

1. It can be based on 12 months, each containing 30 days, with a 360-day year.
2. It can be based on a 365-day year with actual days charged to the buyer.
3. It can be a monthly charge based on the number of days the buyer owns the property.

Prorating should be computed as accurately as possible and can apply to a large number of expenses. For example, if you occupy your home on October 1 and property taxes have been paid up through December 31, you will be prorated part of that expense.

Total property tax bill	$285.60
Total period covered	July 1–Dec. 31
Number of days in period	184
Number of days from 11/1 to 12/31	61
Prorated portion: (61/184) × $285.60 =	$94.68

If utility, water, or refuse bills are prepaid at a set amount, it is possible to compute the daily rate.

Total water and refuse bill per quarter	$31
Current quarter dates	10/1 to 12/31
Number of days in quarter	92
Daily expense	.337 cents
Number of days from 11/1 to 12/31	61
Prorated portion: (61/92) × $31 =	20.55

When your closing date is different from the date when your first mortgage payment will be due, you will be charged for the difference. If you close on November 1 and payments are to begin on December 1, your closing cost for interest will be added.

Mortgage balance	$82,000
Interest rate	11.25%
Interest, full year	$9,225
Due for one month (11/1 through 11/30, assuming use of a 360-day year): (30/360) × $9,225 =	$768.75

THE BUYER'S CLOSING STATEMENT

When the real estate purchase is closed, a statement is issued both to the buyer and the seller. This closing statement summarizes whatever money has been exchanged. A typical buyer's statement will be set up as follows:

BUYER'S CLOSING STATEMENT

Date   November 1, 1987

Property   112 B Street
Elmwood, IL

(Buyer's name)

	Debits	Credits
Purchase price	$90,000.00	
Deposits to escrow		$12,371.98
Loan: First National Savings		82,000.00
Prorated: 11/1 to 12/31		
Property taxes	$94.68	
Utilities	20.55	
Interest	768.75	
Title insurance	250.00	
Escrow fee	85.00	
Inspection report fee	60.00	
Notary fee	4.00	
Recording fee	26.00	
Loan fees	2,700.00	
Tax service fee	33.00	
Credit report	25.00	
Fire insurance, one year	305.00	
Total	94,371.98	$94,371.98

SECTION
II

MORTGAGES

11

SHOPPING FOR A MORTGAGE

Finding the best possible mortgage financing for your new home requires some shopping around. You should become thoroughly familiar with both the range of choices available and the state of the current lending market.

At the time of this writing, mortgage rates have fallen into the single digits, to the lowest levels in more than a decade. When this happens, certainly it is an opportunity for home buyers to obtain a long-term, low-cost mortgage, as it is for present homeowners a chance to refinance a mortgage assumed when interest rates were considerably higher. However, there is no assurance that interest rates will remain low. And there is no sure way to anticipate either an increase or a decrease in home mortgage interest rates.

Like housing prices, the market for money is constantly affected by supply and demand. When money is tight—meaning that too many people are chasing too few available dollars—the lender has a negotiating advantage. The lender can dictate terms, and the buyer has less flexibility in picking the best mortgage financing.

Conversely, when money is not tight—when there is more available to lend than there are borrowers who want it—lenders are naturally motivated to make more attractive mortgage offers. At those times, lenders will offer loans with no points, and at lower interest rates.

PICKING THE RIGHT MORTGAGE

To attract new customers, lenders sometimes offer such inducements as:

1. Lower than current market interest rates
2. Unusual long-term loans
3. Rebates, discounts, and giveaways

Lower interest rates often come with a built-in catch. If you read the fine print, for example, you may discover that the low rates are temporary and that an increase takes effect after one or two years. Adjustable-rate mortgages commonly include this kind of so-called teaser clause.

A loan for a long period of time means lower monthly payments for buyers but a higher interest total paid in the long run. It can mean more flexibility in refinancing later (replacing the loan with another one at more favorable interest rates) and in paying off the loan early (assuming that this prepayment is allowed by the terms of the mortgage contract).

However, if you can afford it, a 15-year mortgage instead of the usual 30-year loan can save you a large amount of money on the cost of the loan. For instance, an $80,000, 12 percent annual interest rate, 15-year loan would require somewhat higher monthly payments than the same loan with a 30-year terms: $960 a month versus $823. But shortening the term of the mortgage loan to 15 years results in a total interest savings of $123,419 over the life of the loan. Since many banks reduce the interest rate slightly because of the 15-year loan's shorter term, you may save even more money in the long run. Even if you take your savings of $137 (realized if you take the 30-year mortgage) and invest it each month, the total interest saved on the 15-year mortgage far outweighs the potential investment income. (See Chapter 13, Mortgage Acceleration, for more details on shorter and longer term mortgages.)

Rebates, discounts, and giveaways are advertising gimmicks. If you are offered a cash rebate or discount or a "prize" for taking out a mortgage loan, you can be sure that the cost is included in your interest rate. Over the years, lenders have developed other variations on the business of lending mortgage money. Look carefully at all the "creative" financing offers made to prospective home buyers. Remember—the lender is in the business of selling you money and the price of that money is interest. Approaching a lender from that point of view will sharpen your awareness of market conditions and make you a more knowledgeable loan applicant.

SOURCES FOR LOANS

Many first-time homebuyers are so pressured by the many complications of the buying process that they fail to shop around sufficiently for a mortgage.

This costly error arises from several misconceptions:

1. That you're lucky to find a lender who will give you a mortgage at all.

2. That there aren't really any choices, as all mortgage loans are essentially the same.

3. That the real estate agent is an expert on mortgage financing and can probably find you the best deal.

First of all, it isn't a matter of luck. Finding a good deal on a mortgage loan, as with any other product of the marketplace, is the result of thoroughly exploring your options. All loans are not the same. The terms of a mortgage contract can and do vary widely among lenders and you won't know what the best deals are unless you compare one with another.

Look for a mortgage loan at lending institutions, including:

SAVINGS AND LOAN ASSOCIATIONS. Responsible for more than half of all mortgage loans in the United States, local savings institutions are the most likely source of mortgage money.

COMMERCIAL BANKS. These banks are chiefly involved in lending money for commercial ventures. However, there are many commercial banks actively engaged in the residential mortgage market.

MORTGAGE BANKERS. A middleman in many mortgage loans, a mortgage banker grants you an original loan and then sells it to another lender.

BUILDERS AND DEVELOPERS. In order to expedite selling a tract of homes, a builder or developer may establish a loan relationship with a lender. The developer can then sell you a home with mortgage financing as part of the deal. Once the loan is granted, it is assigned or sold to the lender. In this way, many home sales are made to first-time buyers that otherwise would not take place.

PRIVATE LOANS. You have the right to get your own loan privately. Such loans have jokingly been called GI loans, since a "good in-law" is most likely to lend you the money.

GOVERNMENT AGENCIES. You can apply for a loan guaranteed by the Veterans Administration and insured by the Federal Housing Administration.

ALTERNATIVE WAYS TO GET A MORTGAGE

Obviously, the stronger your financial position, the more financing choices you will have. Lenders naturally want to place their money with safe and stable borrowers. If your funds are limited, your loan choices will be limited or perhaps even nonexistent unless you're able to offer a sizeable down payment.

You may have an easier time buying and financing a newly built house, where availability of mortgage money is part of the deal. However, terms may not be as favorable as you would like. If this type of home purchase is your only option, we strongly suggest you thoroughly investigate the terms of the deal and be certain that buying a house under these conditions adequately serves your long-term interests. You may decide that it's better to wait.

You may be able to get around the mortgage problem, at least partially, by assuming or taking over an existing mortgage loan on a home. If the seller's mortgage allows a new buyer to assume the loan, it may be a good deal if the interest rate is less than the going interest rates currently being offered by most lenders. However, the rate may be increased by the lender who holds the mortgage, and you still have to meet the lender's credit requirements. (As of this writing, all FHA and VA loans are assumable.) The availability of assumable existing mortgage loans and the conditions of assuming them vary state by state.

THE MORTGAGE SEARCH COMPANY

A relatively new service is gaining in popularity: the mortgage search company. This type of organization, either national or local, uses a computerized network in order to find the best mortgage deals around at any given time.

The mortgage search company agent, armed with a computer printout, can quickly analyze the needs of the borrower, his or her income level and other credentials, and can match them up with the best potential lending sources. The mortgage search company serves a useful function to the lender—worth the commission—by screening out all unlikely mortgage applicants and doing the legwork of processing applications and credit checks. For the borrower, there is a great saving of time and energy—the mortgage search company can find you the best mortgage deal available to you in a comparatively short time.

OTHER CONSIDERATIONS

Choosing the right mortgage means being aware of more than just interest rates. Here are some of the other terms to consider:

POINTS. You may find some lenders offering mortgages for no points and others asking for three or more points. A point is equal to 1 percent of the loan amount and they can add up.

TYPE OF MORTGAGE. You may have the greatest advantage with the longest-term loan at a fixed rate, but lower rates are available if you're willing to settle for an adjustable-rate mortgage. For a discussion of various types of mortgages, see chapter 12.

PREPAYING THE MORTGAGE. Can you pay off the mortgage loan early without penalty? This is sometimes called accelerating the mortgage payment and, while not always recommended, it does reduce the amount of total interest that will eventually be paid on the mortgage. However, every mortgage contract has different restrictions on pay-offs and, depending on your tax bracket and cash flow, it may or may not be right for you. (See chapter 13, Mortgage Acceleration.)

THE LENDER'S DECISION

How do lenders decide to accept or reject an application for a mortgage loan?

It is not an arbitrary decision, although it may appear so to first-time buyers. The process of investigating a loan application is quite thorough and is designed to ensure that the lender takes only a limited amount of risk.

The process is more flexible with some lenders than with others. In a small town, local lenders are more familiar with market values in the various neighborhoods, know the real estate brokers, and may be more willing to underwrite mortgage loans in the community more readily than large, multi-office lenders who handle thousands of loans a year and follow a more regimented, impersonal application procedure.

However, most lenders will not finance more than 80 percent of the current market value of a home. If you want to buy a property valued at $80,000, the maximum loan generally allowed by lenders is $64,000. You must find the money to cover the balance.

Before granting a home mortgage, the lender will check out both the buyer and the property in question, looking carefully at the following:

THE NEIGHBORHOOD. The lender will want information on the neighborhood and its character, including the amount of recent development, the appearance of existing homes, the number of homes currently on the market, and the overall desirability of the area. Lenders also like to know what percentage of homes are occupied by their owners (the higher the better) and how many homes are rented out to tenants.

THE HOUSE. Before granting a mortgage loan for a property, lenders want to obtain an independent appraisal. They also will consider the house's general condition, size and number of rooms, its energy efficiency, and the general quality of its construction. They will also consider the condition of the property itself, general landscaping and appearance and whether or not there are any danger signs, such as evidence of poor drainage, crumbling retaining walls, unsafe location or siting, etc. (In most cases, the applicant for the loan bears the cost of the appraisal.)

YOUR CREDIT RATING. In order to determine your financial history and creditworthiness, lenders will request a credit report, usually from a national agency with offices in various parts of the country. This report is an up-to-date summary of your financial record. It includes any judgments or liens against you or your property, any bankruptcies or previous foreclosures, and any failure to pay debts, such as your record of payments on revolving charge accounts and the like. It's probably a good idea to get a copy of the report of your credit rating before you apply for a mortgage loan. Your lender can give you the name and address of the credit bureau it uses in your area, and you can obtain your credit report for a modest fee.

Other information comes from you and your employer, including your employment record, sources and levels of income, assets, and liabilities. The lender looks for the right combination of financial stability in a mortgage loan applicant, specifically your income and employment profile and your handling of debt.

INCOME AND EMPLOYMENT PROFILE

A successful applicant needs a steady income large enough to support the monthly mortgage payments. Lenders are primarily interested in stable income followed by any secondary income. Stable income includes regularly paid wages. Secondary income—commissions, bonuses, tips, and overtime pay—will impress a lender only if it is related to the occupation of the borrower and has been consistently earned over the last two years.

As a rule, lenders require that your total monthly mortgage payments do not exceed a set pèrcentage of your gross income (that's income before deductions for taxes). They include in this formula not only your principal and interest payments, but amounts withheld for property taxes and homeowner's insurance as well. Most lenders also add to this total any other long-term monthly payments you may be making, such as automobile or personal loan payments, in addition to your monthly mortgage payments. As long as the total of all those payments does not exceed one-third (33 percent) of your total gross income, you should qualify for the mortgage loan. That's the general rule. Some lenders will stretch this percentage to 40 percent, especially in areas where housing prices are high and qualification is difficult for a large number of borrowers. Of course, if you have a sizeable amount of cash in the bank and/or income-producing investments, the lender may bend the rules so you can qualify.

Also, the longer the buyer has been employed by the same employer, the better. Three years or more of steady employment at the same place is reassuring to the lender. If you are self-employed, you will have to provide proof of income to the lender, probably in the form of copies of your federal income tax returns for the last few years.

DEBT MANAGEMENT

Lenders look for a clean credit history with no previous foreclosures on property, no personal bankruptcies or serious criminal records, and a credit history that demonstrates prompt payment on debt.

Lenders look for trouble signs. For example, if the credit report discloses one or more debts the borrower failed to list on the loan application, the lender may conclude that the borrower has something to hide.

A borrower who has been through a bankruptcy or a previous foreclosure on a home must be able to demonstrate several years of consistently responsible financial performance or the lender will almost certainly turn down the application. In such cases, most lenders will take extra care to examine both the home buyer's past financial problems and recent credit history before making a final judgment.

If you possess good lines of credit—for example, charge cards—that's a sign that other lenders have faith in your ability to handle debt. However, some lenders will view them skeptically, especially if you tend to accumulate debt without any evidence of a growing net worth. In some cases, the lender may request that the applicant close certain open lines of credit. The lender may fear that a first-time home buyer, without visible assets (including furniture and cars) may build up a dangerously high level of consumer debt after the purchase of the house and eventually may not be able to meet the monthly mortgage payment.

Applicants must supply proof of a viable and growing net worth and evidence of a responsible attitude toward money management. This includes the ability to acquire and conserve assets and keep debt within reasonable limits. Assets are divided into two categories: liquid and all other. Liquid assets include cash, savings, and investments or accounts receivable that can be converted to cash in a short period of time. Nonliquid assets include cars, furniture, boats, artwork, jewelry, etc.

Liabilities have similar characteristics. Some liabilities, such as previous loans, may fall due in the near future. So lenders are especially interested in the comparison between liquid assets and current liabilities. The question is how well the borrower will be able to handle current obligations from liquid assets that are available; lenders apply ratios between assets and liabilities to arrive at a judgment of financial strength. This difference between assets and liabilities is called net worth. Most lenders agree that the ability to accumulate net worth over time is a strong indication of creditworthiness.

Of course, a lender who is willing to work with you closely can be of enormous help in obtaining a mortgage loan. A conscientious loan officer recognizes the benefit of working with the home buyer, ensuring that the financial commitment about to be made is understood completely in all its long-term ramifications. The ultimate disaster—losing your home because you can't keep up the mortgage loan payments—means that everyone loses, both buyer and lender. Most lenders would prefer not to have to foreclose on a house.

In summary, if you look at the process of applying for a mortgage loan as a passive one—out of your control and entirely up to a loan officer—communication will be poor and you won't do much shopping around for a better deal elsewhere. Ideally, a long-term mortgage loan arrangement is a partnership between lender and borrower. Both sides share a common goal and understand fully the rights and obligations of both parties—the home buyer successfully pays off his mortgage loan while enjoying the benefits of home ownership, and the lender generates local goodwill and a profit on his money at the same time.

12

INTEREST AND MORTGAGES

Lending money is a business like any other. Money is its product. Lenders buy and sell money, take their losses and pay their expenses, and hope to make a worthwhile profit.

Just as a store owner purchases goods to sell to the public, the lender must pay a price for the money he or she makes available for mortgages. The store owner adjusts the price of goods according to what they cost him. When the owner's costs go up, his retail prices increase as well.

Interest is the cost of borrowed money. The rate a lender will charge on new loans will fluctuate according to changes in the cost of money to the lender.

Where do lenders get money? Savings and loan associations, which make most mortgage loans, have two types of customers: savers (who supply the money) and borrowers (who take out loans).

The rate of interest the savings institution pays to its savers is the "cost of money" to the institution. This is paid out through passbook savings accounts, time deposits, and other interest-bearing accounts. If the average rate paid to savers is 8 percent and the institution has determined it must take in 4 percent more than it pays (this is called the *spread*), the cost to borrowers will be 12 percent:

Cost of money (average rate paid to savers)	8%
Gross profit requirement (the spread)	4%
Average mortgage rate	12%

The spread isn't all profit. That 4 percent must also cover overhead expenses such as salaries, rent, and taxes as well as the estimated cost of defaulted loans.

COMPUTING INTEREST

There are a number of ways a lender can compute interest on a mortgage loan. The more creative methods can spell trouble for a homeowner who does not understand the fine print clearly.

The fully "amortized," or periodically reduced, loan is the standard type of mortgage in use today. The payment you make each month is calculated to pay off the entire loan within a specified number of years. Interest is computed each month on the balance of the mortgage and is "front-end loaded" so most of the interest is paid off in the early years.

You can see how high the cost of interest is by figuring out how much money will be paid off over a 30-year period. For example, a $50,000 loan at 13 percent paid over 30 years costs $553.10 per month. That adds up to $199,116, of which $149,116 is interest.

Because full amortization based on monthly payments involves dividing the nominal annual rate by 12, you actually pay a higher rate. Using 13 percent as an example, the annual percentage rate (APR) actually is 13.803 percent. This can be computed by multiplying one-twelfth of the annual rate by itself 12 times.

One-twelfth of 13 percent is 0.0108333. Multiply, adding 1 to the factor for each month to arrive at the APR. Thus, 1.0108333 is each month's multiplier:

Month	Compounded Rate
1	1.083%
2	2.178
3	3.285
4	4.404
5	5.535
6	6.679
7	7.834
8	9.002
9	10.183
10	11.377
11	12.584
12	13.803

When a rate of interest is advertised, the Federal Truth in Lending Law requires disclosure of the APR. Ads usually will express the interest rate like this: "13% (13.803% APR)."

THE MORTGAGE

A mortgage is a lien, or claim, against a piece of property that is being purchased. The real estate is collateral for that loan. If the buyer fails to make timely payments on the loan, the lender can foreclose and take the house away.

Houses are purchased in one of four ways:

1. With cash. No mortgage is needed because the buyer has enough cash to pay for the entire property.

2. With a conventional loan. A down payment is made, and financing is obtained through a mortgage from a lender, usually a savings and loan association or a bank.

3. With a government-backed loan. A government-guaranteed or government-insured loan is obtained, often for little or nothing down.

4. With an assumed mortgage. An existing mortgage on the property is taken over by the buyer from the seller.

Financing also can consist of a combination of these methods. If a lender requires a 20 percent down payment on a home but you don't have enough cash, it may be possible to take out a second mortgage. However, many lenders may refuse to issue a first mortgage if they know you are resorting to a second mortgage in order to swing the deal. The second mortgage can, of course, be obtained from a private source, such as a relative or friend.

FIXED VERSUS ADJUSTABLE LOANS

The most popular forms of mortgage lending in use today are the fixed-rate mortgage and the adjustable-rate mortgage (ARM).

After weighing all the factors, the home buyer must decide which type of mortgage is better for him or her.

A *fixed-rate* mortgage—the traditional form of lending that has been in use for hundreds of years—is one in which your required monthly payment never varies. Regardless of whether interest rates go up or down, your rate is fixed. It can be changed during the mortgage period only if you cancel the loan and take out another. An *adjustable-rate* mortgage (ARM) is one in which interest payments change periodically, usually every year or two, depending on the agreement. The change is based on interest rate changes in a specified index. Different lenders use different indexes, including the interest rates on U.S. Treasury securities and state and national inflation indexes.

ARM contracts have been in common use only since the early 1980s. However, the Federal National Mortgage Association (more popularly known as "Fannie Mae," and a government-created corporation whose purpose is to make mortgage money available to low- and moderate-income home buyers) reports that more than half of all new home sales were financed by adjustable-rate mortgages by the end of 1984.

Can you predict how volatile interest rates will be? You can't. So some safeguards—as well as traps—are built into an ARM loan contract.

An adjustable-rate mortgage, because it involves more risk, will be generally more available at a lower initial rate than a fixed-rate mortgage. However, there is no guarantee that the rate will remain lower over the entire loan period.

Deciding which kind of mortgage is better for you depends on how long you plan to stay in your house, your income level, and the amount of risk you're willing to take. Most indexes used by ARM lenders are likely to remain fairly stable within a five-year period. Thus you can be fairly sure, at least for that amount of time, that the loan will cost you less in most cases than a fixed-rate mortgage.

It is too early in the history of ARM contracts to spot strong trends in the movement of rates tied to an index, or to recommend one index over another. The smart home buyer considering an adjustable-rate mortgage should certainly review the movement of the specified index used by your lender for the last five years or so before agreeing to a mortgage contract. The Sunday New York Times, Wall Street Journal, and other financial journals are a good source of information on the weekly average yields of such indexes. Consult your local library for other sources of information.

If your lender's index exhibits extremely volatile movement—swings of more than two percentage points within a one-year period—or rapid climbs in rates, chances are that it may well exhibit the same volatility in the future. Seek a lender who bases an ARM mortgage contract on a more stable index, such as the one-year Treasury index.

An ARM is most advantageous when:

1. You will stay in your house no more than five years.

2. You cannot meet the qualifications for a fixed-rate mortgage at current rates, based on your level of income. However, in this case the risk is that the interest on an ARM contract will rise beyond your ability to meet future payments. Be sure that you can afford the largest possible payment of an ARM contract before agreeing to its terms.

3. Your income is rising or expected to rise to the point where making increasing monthly mortgage payments will not be much of a problem.

4. The index rates used by the lender haven't changed dramatically in recent years.

5. The contract includes a ceiling, or cap, on the rate of interest you can be charged, regardless of how high the index moves, or how often your rate can be increased. A rate cap is better than a payment cap, which often leads to negative amortization—a situation in which, as time passes, the full balance due becomes greater than the original amount of the loan. (More details on negative amortization are found later in this chapter.)

A fixed-rate mortgage is generally a better choice. It is especially preferable when:

1. You plan to remain in your house longer than five years.

2. Your income is fixed or rises slowly.

3. A fixed housing cost is important to you, and you're willing to start out with a higher rate of interest in return.

4. The terms of ARM contracts you review are too vague or too generous to the lender, or no caps are placed on the maximum amount of interest the lender is allowed to charge.

TOTAL INTEREST COSTS

The type of mortgage loan you select can have a great effect on how much interest you pay over the life of the loan. With a fixed-rate loan, you start out with a higher rate. But if interest rates gradually increase and exceed your fixed rate, you eventually will have a real bargain.

If interest rates remain below the rate you are paying, you are paying a premium for the use of money. If interest rates appear stable or dropping, it may be worthwhile to look for another fixed-rate loan at the lower rate. There will be a penalty involved in canceling one mortgage and replacing it with another, but if you plan to remain in your house for many years, it will pay off. Certainly, if rates drop 3% or more, you should refinance.

An adjustable-rate mortgage can end up being much more expensive than a fixed-rate mortgage if interest rates go up. You could get to the maximum within several years and be required to pay much more than the rate you started out with. Even a slight rise in interest rates can add substantially to your monthly costs.

Many people enter an ARM contract with the idea of later replacing it with a fixed-rate mortgage, depending on the movement of interest rates.

That's fine, as long as rates decline. If they climb, you'll be paying a high rate of interest in the ARM contract, and refinancing will be equally expensive.

For example, if you enter an ARM contract that begins at 10 percent annual interest and fixed rates are running 12 percent, you're ahead. On an $80,000 loan to be repaid over 30 years, you're saving about $120 a month. But if the contract sets a ceiling at 15 percent, your monthly payment ultimately could climb a staggering $410 which is more than a 50 percent increase.

In the recent past, when interest rates soared and people were not buying houses, some lenders tried to drum up business by allowing home buyers who could not otherwise qualify for a loan to essentially "rent" one for a few years, paying interest only. The entire balance was due in three or four years. This is called a *balloon payment*.

The argument in favor of balloon payments is that property values will rise, giving more equity to a borrower who otherwise would never be able to afford a home. When the balloon loan comes due, another loan, theoretically, may be arranged.

The unfortunate reality was that many people hoping to eventually own their homes ended up losing them. They had paid high rates for several years, gained little or no equity, and ended up where they began, or worse off for the experience.

Balloon payment loans are less common today than they were a few years ago, when it was difficult for many people to qualify for a less "creative" kind of loan.

THE ADJUSTABLE-RATE MORTGAGE

The ARM, as previously stated, is a contract in which the interest rate changes periodically according to a specific index that is identified by the lender when the loan agreement is signed.

This type of loan was developed when interest rates jumped significantly in the late 1970s. Until 1972, rates were dependably low, averaging 7 percent or less on home mortgages. From 1972 through 1980, rates soared, at one point reaching more than 20 percent.

During that time, lenders were carrying many mortgage loans that had been issued years earlier at fixed rates that were much lower. Meanwhile, they were also paying savers at high rates. So they moved to share some of their risks with consumers by creating a mortgage in which the interest rate was variable instead of fixed. Lenders, particularly savings and loan associations, suffered large losses.

Adjustable-rate mortgages can be obtained for a 30-year term, although many are written for 15 years only. Some ARM contracts will specify the maximum and minimum loan terms. If rates change drastically but there are limits (caps) on the monthly payment or on the rate that can be charged, the lender may specify that the loan must be paid off by a certain date.

PROS AND CONS OF THE ARM CONTRACT

Some would-be home buyers simply cannot qualify for a fixed-rate loan, usually because their income is too low. For example, a lender's policy may stipulate that your monthly gross income (the amount you make before federal and state taxes are taken out) must average three times the amount of your mortgage payment.

Let's say that you're interested in a $40,000 loan at 13 percent to be repaid over 30 years. Your monthly income is only $1,200. You need $1,327 to qualify. In this case, the lender could reject your fixed-rate loan but offer you an 11 percent ARM in which monthly payments would be only $380.93.

Another benefit of many ARM contracts is that lower down payments are required because the lender's long-term risks are lower. For those unable to raise the conventional 20 percent or 25 percent down payment, this can be a big plus.

The major disadvantage of an ARM is that your payment is not permanently set for the loan period. If rates climb, so will your payments. This can add up if rates increase quickly. In our example the starting payment of $380.93 on a $40,000 loan over 30 years beginning at 11 percent can change drastically over time:

Rate %	Monthly Payment
11	$380.93
12	411.45
13	442.48
14	473.95
15	505.78
16	537.91

The difference of roughly $30 per month for each percentage point can add up if rates continue to climb during the years when you're paying off the mortgage on your house.

RATE AND PAYMENT CAPS

Safeguards can be built into an ARM contract to limit the possible increase in rate and costs. However, not all caps are designed to protect you.

Some forms of caps can work against you by boosting monthly payments or adding to your interest cost over time.

The *rate cap* is a limit on the percentage of interest or on the amount by which the interest rate can be increased in a given year. There are two types of rate caps, both of which can be included in the same agreement:

1. A cap on annual increase. This limits the rise in interest each year. If a contract specifies that the rate cannot increase by more than 1 percent a year, you have limited protection. Be sure to read the entire provision in the mortgage contract. The lender may reserve the right to carry over any rate increase exceeding 1 percent. This means that the following year you could also have a 1 percent increase even if the index had gone down.

2. A cap on any overall increase. This sets a limit on the rate that can be charged over the entire contract period. An ARMs contract written at 11 percent may include the provision that the maximum rate that can be charged at any time is 16 percent. Again, you have to read the fine print.

The following example tells why: The index exceeds 16 percent, but your interest rate is frozen there. The following year, the index moves back down below the 16 percent level. However, the terms of the mortgage contract specify that you must continue paying 16 percent until you catch up with the excess. The contract may also call for a minimum interest rate to be charged. In that case you still will be charged a minimum rate of interest, even if the index falls below a specified level. When you examine a mortgage loan's caps, check carefully to see whether they are calculated on the initial interest rate, or based on the index rate. The two are not always the same, and if you don't check, you may find out later that the cap is pitched higher than you assumed.

The *payment cap* is potentially more troublesome for the home buyer entering an ARM contract.

This payment cap clause states that you will never be required to pay more than a specified amount each month on your mortgage. Although this sounds very reassuring, it's really a deceptive statement. In this case, the loan officer tells you: "I assure you, with absolute certainty, that your monthly payment will never be more than $850 per month."

What the loan officer doesn't tell you is that if the interest rate rises, more of your monthly payment will be going toward interest and not toward paying off the principal loan. For example, if your loan balance is $63,000 at 13 percent, $682.50 of your monthly payment is for interest. The difference of $105 is what is now *not* going toward paying off your actual loan.

NEGATIVE AMORTIZATION

In an extreme case, you could end up in the situation known as "negative amortization." This means that, even though you are making the maximum monthly payments on your mortgage, the actual balance of the loan is going up instead of down. This occurs largely during times of rising interest rates and because the capped payment is not high enough to completely cover the monthly interest based on the index specified in the contract. As long as that index calls for an interest rate that is higher than your maximum payment can cover, your loan balance grows because none of the principal is being paid off and the unpaid interest is adding to the balance.

In some cases, your loan term will be lengthened to allow you more time to pay the debt—but of course this means you'll pay even more interest than you had originally planned on. In other cases, you'll owe a large sum at the end of the mortgage term.

Why do some ARM mortgage contracts include this payment cap provision if it eventually may result in such a dangerous situation for the buyer? Largely because such a provision alleviates the fears many buyers have about being able to afford the monthly payments. It gives a false sense of security to the mortgagee about his or her future mortgage liability.

You can prevent negative amortization in your ARM mortgage contract by insisting on an ARM with both a yearly and a life-of-the-contract *rate* cap. This provision will limit the maximum monthly payment and avoid the build-up of unpaid interest charges which may come with only a payment cap to protect you in the future.

If you enter an ARM contract with only a payment cap and the interest rate specified in your index goes up to the point of negative amortization, what can you do? First, you can try to negotiate a new mortgage that includes a rate cap instead of a payment cap, although this may be difficult to do during times of rising interest rates. Second, if at all possible, you should prepay enough of the mortgage balance to take it below the negative amortization point. Even if this remedy requires your taking out a second mortgage, you will be better off than you would be if you allowed the balance of the loan to rise each month.

THE TEASER

Advertisements for some ARMs boast about the extremely low interest rate offered. Some lending institutions euphemistically call this teaser clause the "today rate." What isn't advertised is the fact that this very low rate will end in a year or two.

Say you begin the ARM contract with payments based on a 9 percent rate, at a time when most ARM contracts are being offered at 11 percent, and fixed-rate mortgages are going for 13 percent. The ads may have promised the "lowest rates possible" or something equally persuasive.

You will discover, however, that the 9 percent rate is good for only 12 to 24 months. After that, the rate automatically goes up to 11 percent or more.

Some teasers are even more deceiving. You may be required to make up the interest lost because of the lower teaser rate. After two years, for example, you may find that one of the following will occur:

1. The rate jumps to a point higher than other ARM mortgages to make up for the lower rate you have been paying. In this case, your monthly payment jumps, too. If you agree to a loan with a teaser of 10 percent, which later goes to 13 percent, the difference will be substantial. On a 30-year loan for $80,000, the jump will amount to $182 more in payments every month. '

2. An adjustment is made in your balance for interest accrued during the first two years. This means that it will take longer to pay off your loan, and more of your monthly payment will go toward interest. It also means you have qualified for a loan you may not be able to afford.

A lender should explain the complicated provisions of an ARM contract to you in detail. An honest lender will want to make sure that you know exactly what you're getting into. But with the pressure to make money and compete for mortgage loan business, some loan officers have failed the public in this regard. If you can't get satisfactory answers to your questions about an ARM contract, pay for an attorney's review or shop elsewhere.

THE FIXED-RATE MORTGAGE

The traditional home mortgage, which nearly everyone had until the 1970s, has a fixed rate of interest.

There is an all-important advantage to this type of mortgage: Payments never change as long as the mortgage stays in effect. If you can qualify for a fixed-rate mortgage with payments you can afford, you have three things going for you.

1. You enjoy the financial security of knowing that your housing cost is fixed for many years to come.

2. You have the flexibility to keep or replace the mortgage. If you later find a cheaper loan that also offers fixed interest, you can refinance your mortgage, but if interest rates go up, you can keep the mortgage at its fixed cost.

3. Your cost burden is actually likely to go down. Assuming that your income will increase to keep up with inflation over several decades, the fixed costs of housing should become a smaller percentage of your total earnings.

There are some disadvantages to fixed-rate mortgages. One of the greatest is that many home buyers cannot qualify.

1. They cannot come up with enough cash for the required down payment, which is higher for most fixed-rate mortgages than it is for ARMs. Most fixed-rate mortgage agreements will cover 80 percent of a home's cost, and so a down payment of 20 percent is required. Some lenders may require 25 percent or even 30 percent down.

2. Their income ·is not high enough to meet the lender's standards for fixed-rate financing.

Another disadvantage can be the interest rate itself. Fixed-rate loans are given at a higher rate—usually 1 to 2 percent higher—than ARMs. This is because the lender takes a greater risk by fixing the interest rate for as long as three decades.

The fixed rate becomes a problem only if interest rates decrease several points over the years. This is a minor problem for those homeowners who prefer to know exactly what their payments will be each month. Their lack of worry about fluctuating ARM interest rates is worth the extra cost.

NEGOTIATING

If you decide that a fixed-rate mortgage is what you want, and market conditions allow, you can try to negotiate the following with your lender:

1. The amount of down payment required
2. The interest rate charged
3. The number of points you will pay

Keep in mind that the lender prefers to sell you an ARM. However, the lender's terms for fixed-rate mortgages aren't necessarily carved in stone. Whether there is room for negotiation depends on current supply and demand: Does the lender need your business, or does he or she have many customers clamoring for a limited amount of lendable money?

You can tell what the mortgage market is like by checking out the ads on the radio and in the newspapers. When lenders are looking for borrowers, they offer no-point loans, free appraisals and so on. When lenders are not seeking more business, you literally will be turned away. They don't want your business when interest rates are too low relative to the cost of funds, or when most lenders are overextended in the mortgage market.

When business is slow for the lender, you will have a better chance of negotiating successfully. You may be charged fewer points or perhaps even a lower rate. You also may be able to persuade the lender to carry a higher percentage of the total purchase price. If a 25 percent down payment is required, ask to be granted the loan with only 20 percent down. If your credit is strong, you may get your way. Of course, you may have to pay more interest in that case.

HOW THE NEW TAX LAW AFFECTS THE HOME BUYER

Under the Tax Reform Act of 1986 you may deduct all interest on the mortgage loan you use to purchase your primary (and one designated secondary) residence, up to the fair market value of each property. Therefore, every home buyer taking out a mortgage loan to finance a new home is able generally to deduct all the interest charges on that loan.

Of course, because of the lower tax rates, the mortgage-interest deduction, like all other deductions, is worth less to the taxpayer—the after-tax costs of owning a home will increase. But this in turn may slow down the growth in existing home prices, and help to maintain home owning as a principal source of tax benefits.

If you have refinanced or negotiated for a second mortgage on your home, you are protected by a transitional rule that allows you to deduct all the interest on a mortgage loan obtained on or before August 16, 1986. If you refinanced or got a second mortgage on your home after that date, or if you are doing so on a home purchased after that date, you may deduct only the loan interest which does not exceed a threshold amount. That is, the threshold must equal the sum of your adjusted basis which is the original cost of the home plus the cost of your improvements, plus the amount of any portion of your mortgage loan that you use to pay for medical or educational expenses for you, your spouse, or dependents. (Such expenses must be paid or incurred within a reasonable time before or after the loan is obtained.) Therefore, under this rule, a deduction is still allowed for mortgage loans obtained for the purpose of making home improvements.

VARIATIONS ON FINANCING

Not every mortgage loan's terms necessarily conform to the simple straight monthly payment, or to the conventional 15- or 30-year term, or even to the established rate policies. These variations, or so-called "creative" financing, are popular during times of tight money and high interest rates, and usually disappear during days of easy money and ready mortgage availability. But such difficult financial times may return, so we include these mortgage variations here.

GRADUATED-PAYMENT MORTGAGE. This is a mortgage designed for those who expect to be able to afford larger payments in the future. Monthly payments increase at preset intervals, usually five to ten years. However, the interest rate remains the same. This means that the loan balance will actually increase during the early years, as the payment can't cover interest; the excess is added to the loan balance each month. This is a form of negative amortization.

For example, you take out an $80,000 loan at 12 percent interest. Over a normal 30-year term, your payments would be $822.90 per month, but under a graduated-payment loan, you start out paying only $700. However, the first month's interest is $800, a full $100 higher than your payment. The loan balance will go up accordingly.

After five years, the loan balance has grown to $88,165. Payments at that point will graduate to $929 per month: the amount required to pay off the entire balance in the remaining 25 years of the 30-year term.

ROLLOVER MORTGAGE. Also called the *renegotiable-rate mortgage*, this is a financing arrangement in which the interest rate and payment remain fixed for a specified period, commonly three to five years. At the end of that time, the terms are renegotiated.

Depending on the volatility of the interest market at that time as well as the going rate for mortgage loans, the lender can offer to roll over the loan at a higher or a lower rate.

BALLOON MORTGAGE. Monthly payments are made at level rates and often consist of interest only. A large—balloon—payment is due at the end of the term, which is often as short as three to five years from the date of the agreement. The lender often will guarantee refinancing but not the interest rate that will be charged.

SHARED-APPRECIATION MORTGAGE. The mortgage is granted at an interest rate below the market rate. In exchange, a portion of any profits on the property will belong to the lender. This portion can be as high as 30 to 50 percent. In some contracts, it is payable only upon sale; in others, it is due after a specified number of years, whether the house has been sold or not, and is based on current market value.

Consider the former type: payable upon sale. Say the lender is entitled to 30 percent of the profits on a home purchased for $100,000. A few years later, you sell the house for $130,000. The lender will receive $9,000 in addition to the balance of proceeds due on the loan.

In the latter, more common type—with the shared appreciation due within a few years—the lender will be entitled to a portion of the increased market value. Your house will be appraised to set the market value at that point. If it has appreciated by $30,000, the lender will be due $9,000. If you do not have the cash, you have to borrow the money. At that point, the loan can be renegotiated or can continue at its below-market rate.

SHARED-EQUITY MORTGAGE. An investor helps the buyer with the down payment, monthly payments, or both; in return, the investor either owns a portion of the house or is entitled to a share of profits upon sale. The buyer may also be required to pay rent to the investor for the portion of the house that is subsidized.

Say you purchase a house for $100,000, taking out an $80,000 mortgage. For the balance, a friend puts up $10,000 and you match it. This represents a 10 percent shared equity. You may be required to pay 10 percent of the going rate for rentals in the area and also to pay out 10 percent of your profits upon sale.

WRAPAROUND MORTGAGE. Sometimes called all-inclusive mortgages, wraparounds are most common on the West Coast. Essentially a form of second mortgage, wraparounds are complicated procedures, and the buyer and lender should get expert legal advice before entering into such an arrangement.

Essentially, the buyer assumes a low-interest mortgage held by the seller as part of the purchase price. The balance of the price is covered with a new higher-rate mortgage. Both contracts are combined, and the interest rate is the average rate of the two mortgages.

Let's use an example to illustrate: You're buying a $100,000 house and the going rate of mortgages in your area is 12 percent. But the seller has an assumable existing loan on the property at 9 percent with a balance of $30,000 outstanding. Your new loan is granted at 12 percent and with a balance of $50,000. Combining both these loans in a wraparound mortgage means the buyer would have an $80,000 mortgage loan with a weighted average interest rate of 10.875 percent.

BUY-DOWN MORTGAGE. A buyer who cannot qualify for a mortgage loan at current rates is given one with a lower rate for the first two to five years. The difference is paid by a developer or home builder. After the low-rate term, a higher interest rate takes effect. The amount paid by the builder probably will be reflected in a higher purchase price.

An example: A $100,000 home normally will be financed with a 20 percent down payment and an $80,000 loan at 12 percent. In a buy-down, the buyer is initially charged 10 percent, but the price of the home is raised to $115,000, with 20 percent ($23,000) down and an 80 percent ($92,000) mortgage. The 10 percent rate will apply for the first five years of the mortgage. After that, the loan must be renegotiated. The developer receives an additional $15,000 and pays the lender the additional 2 percent, or $137.96 a month. Over five years, the developer pays a total of $8,277.60.

GROWING-EQUITY MORTGAGE. This is also called a *rapid-payoff mortgage*. Payments increase each year, with the entire increment going toward the loan balance. Consequently, the loan is paid off more quickly than with a standard contract.

Under this arrangement, your rate is fixed. Thus, on an $80,000 mortgage at 12 percent, the normal monthly payment for a 30-year loan ($822.90) may increase by $75 per month every two years until the eighth year:

Years 1 and 2	$822.90
Years 3 and 4	897.90
Years 5 and 6	972.90
Years 7 and 8	1,047.90
Years 9 and beyond	1,122.90

The number of years required to pay off the loan are substantially reduced. In one variation on this idea, the homeowner makes two payments a month, one of which goes entirely toward the principal. In this case, the mortgage will be paid off in about five and one-half years.

REVERSE-ANNUITY MORTGAGE. A reverse-annuity mortgage (RAM) is granted to those who own their homes free of a mortgage and want a regular monthly income but do not want to take out a mortgage and make monthly payments. Usually the homeowner must be over age 65. Payments are made by the lender to the owner every month. Each payment adds to the outstanding RAM balance, with interest calculated and added on. These payments can be guaranteed for life or for a specified number of years. The lender is repaid when this period expires, the owner dies, or the house is sold. If the loan must be repaid when the period expires, the borrower may be forced to sell the house and move in order to pay off the loan. (In banking parlance, this is called "getting rammed.")

A person aged 65 with a house worth $100,000 receives approximately $600 per month in a typical RAM arrangement.

GOVERNMENT MORTGAGES

A number of federal agencies offer mortgages to home buyers who meet special requirements.

VA MORTGAGE. The Veterans Administration grants loans to veterans and to the qualified widows of veterans. Also called the GI mortgage, this loan usually is guaranteed at a fixed interest rate that is lower than current market rates. VA mortgages require minimal down payments, and in some cases, no down payment. There is no prepayment penalty, and a VA mortgage can be assumed by a subsequent buyer. The term is 30 years.

The loan is granted by a savings and loan association or other conventional lender but is guaranteed by the federal government—thus the lower rates and more favorable terms.

Not every conventional lender will participate in VA mortgages, and so outlets are limited. The approval period is unusually long, since the loan must be cleared through the VA.

To find out whether you qualify, order the VA's free booklet by writing to the Veterans Administration, 810 Vermont Avenue, N.W., Washington DC 20420. Or phone 202-389-2741.

FHA MORTGAGE. The Federal Housing Administration (FHA) grants mortgages similar to the VA loans. The FHA insures mortgages granted by commercial lenders for loan applicants who would not otherwise qualify. FHA mortgages also feature a low down payment, a 30-year term, no prepayment penalty, and possibly a lower than market interest rate.

Like VA mortgages, FHA loans are granted by a conventional lender but are federally insured. Before the loan is granted, the house and property in question must pass inspection by an FHA official.

Again, approval takes time, and not all conventional lenders participate. The FHA publishes an information booklet on its mortgage loan program. Write to the Federal Housing Adminstration, Washington DC 20410.

FARMERS HOME ADMINISTRATION. The FmHA grants a smaller number of loans. The buyer must live in a rural area (though he or she doesn't have to be a farmer) and must be unable to qualify for a conventional loan. Annual income must be below a level established by the FmHA.

These loans require little or nothing down, can be paid off with a term as long as 33 years, and are offered at below-market interest rates. Write to the Farmers Home Administration, Agriculture Building, Washington DC 20250. Or phone 202-447-7967.

MONTHLY MORTGAGE PAYMENT TABLES

You can estimate your monthly mortgage payment for principal and interest by referring to the following tables. Note that impounds for property taxes, homeowner's insurance, and other types of insurance are *not* included.

Find the interest rate you expect to pay in the far left column. If your rate falls in between—if you'll be paying 9 3/4 percent, for example—you can estimate the monthly payment as being approximately halfway between the payment amount for those rates immmediately below and above.

Three columns—one each for 15, 25, and 30 years—are included so that you can compare the total monthly mortgage payment you would be making for each of those specific mortgage amortization terms.

There are four different tables, one each for $75,000, $100,000, $125,000 and $150,000 loans. You can estimate the payment you will have to make for an amount in between by adding to the tables. For example, if your mortgage will be $110,000, check table II ($100,000). Add 10 percent to the amount shown for $100,000. If your loan is 9 percent and you will be paying over 30 years, payments would be $804.63. To compute payments for $110,000 mortgage, add 10 percent to that amount:

$$\begin{array}{r} \$804.63 \\ +80.46 \\ \hline \$885.09 \end{array}$$

Consult your lender for more detailed information about the level of loan mortgage payments. You can also buy more complete loan amortization table books in most bookstores.

TABLE 12.1. $75,000 MORTGAGE

	Mortgage Term, $/Month		
rate, %	15 years	25 years	30 years
8	716.74	578.87	550.33
8½	738.56	603.93	576.69
9	760.70	629.40	603.47
9½	783.17	655.28	630.65
10	805.96	681.53	658.18
10½	829.05	708.14	686.06
11	852.45	735.09	714.25
11½	876.15	762.36	742.72
12	900.13	789.92	771.46
12½	924.40	817.77	800.45
13	948.94	845.88	829.65
13½	973.74	874.24	859.06
14	998.81	902.83	888.66

TABLE 12.2. $100,000 MORTGAGE

	Mortgage Term, $/Month		
rate, %	15 years	25 years	30 years
8	955.66	771.82	733.77
8½	984.74	805.23	768.92
9	1,014.27	839.20	804.63
9½	1,044.23	873.70	840.86
10	1,074.61	908.71	877.58
10½	1,105.40	944.19	914.74
11	1,136.60	980.12	952.33
11½	1,168.19	1,016.47	990.30
12	1,200.17	1,053.23	1,028.62
12½	1,232.53	1,090.36	1,067.26
13	1,265.25	1,127.84	1,106.20
13½	1,298.32	1,165.65	1,145.42
14	1,331.75	1,203.77	1,184.88

TABLE 12.3. $125,000 MORTGAGE

	Mortgage Term, $/Month		
rate, %	15 years	25 years	30 years
8	1,194.58	964.78	917.22
8½	1,230.93	1,006.54	961.15
9	1,267.84	1,049.00	1,005.79
9½	1,305.29	1,092.13	1,051.08
10	1,343.27	1,135.89	1,096.98
10½	1,381.75	1,180.24	1,143.43
11	1,420.75	1,225.15	1,190.42
11½	1,460.24	1,270.59	1,237.88
12	1,500.22	1,316.54	1,285.78
12½	1,540.67	1,362.95	1,334.08
13	1,581.57	1,409.80	1,382.75
13½	1,622.90	1,457.07	1,431.78
14	1,664.69	1,504.72	1,481.10

TABLE 12.4. $150,000 MORTGAGE

	Mortgage Term, $/Month		
rate, %	15 years	25 years	30 years
8	1,433.49	1,157.73	1,100.66
8½	1,477.11	1,207.85	1,153.38
9	1,521.41	1,258.80	1,206.65
9½	1,566.35	1,310.55	1,261.29
10	1,611.92	1,363.07	1,316.37
10½	1,658.10	1,416.29	1,372.11
11	1,704.90	1,470.18	1,428.50
11½	1,752.29	1,524.71	1,485.45
12	1,800.26	1,579.85	1,542.93
12½	1,848.80	1,635.54	1,600.89
13	1,897.88	1,691.76	1,659.30
13½	1,947.48	1,748.48	1,718.13
14	1,997.63	1,805.67	1,777.32

13

MORTGAGE ACCELERATION PROGRAMS

At this point you will have seen how small a portion of your monthly mortgage payments actually goes toward paying off the cost of your home, so you can understand why your balance creeps downward as slowly as it does. However, there are ways you can pay off a mortgage more quickly than is required, and in the process save yourself a good deal of money.

This prepayment plan is called mortgage acceleration, and the reasoning behind it is the simple fact that since interest represents a major portion of the monthly payment, especially in the first few years, by paying off more of the principal each month you can slash the total cost of your investment. Simply add an extra amount to the monthly mortgage payment in months when you can afford to. Mark the extra payment "for principal only." Most lenders permit you to do that, but check in advance to be sure the terms of your mortgage allow you to make the extra payments without incurring prepayment penalties. Of course, the earlier and more often you make these payments, the greater your savings will be. (For further details see "How Mortgage Acceleration Works" later on in this chapter.)

DRAWBACKS OF ACCELERATION

You can view an acceleration plan as a forced savings account. You will gain by the amount of interest you save and the equity that is rapidly building up. However, the money is not as available to you as it would be in a savings account at a bank down the street. (The resulting equity can be borrowed, but that is a complicated process, requiring a mortgage loan with all the related closing costs, credit checks, and delays.) For your own peace of mind, be sure the money you're putting in a mortgage acceleration program is money you won't need for several years.

Another drawback is that mortgage acceleration may run counter to the normal needs of a household budget. Before beginning such a savings program, make sure you have a savings account large enough to cover household emergencies. Many financial experts suggest that a family have six months' income put away as an emergency fund. Others consider three months' income to be generally adequate. Decide for yourself how much is necessary for you and your family—if your car breaks down, will you be able to come up with several hundred dollars for repairs? More drastically, if you lose your job tomorrow, how long will it take you to find another, and how will you subsist until then?

IS A SHORTER TERM MORTGAGE THE ANSWER?

Another way to achieve mortgage acceleration is to take a shorter term mortgage in the first place. Taking 15 years to pay o ff a loan, instead of 30, will lower your total interest costs substantially, if you can afford to make the higher monthly payments required.

TABLE 13.1. $50,000 FIXED-RATE MORTGAGE

Interest rate	30 years mortgage	15 years mortgage	Difference in dollars	Percentage difference
8%	$367	$478	$111	30%
10	439	537	98	22
12	514	600	86	17
14	592	666	74	13

In 1985 Consumer Reports suggested that taxes saved on a 30-year mortgage along with the saving on monthly payments compared with a 15-year loan, is money that people in the higher tax bracket could be investing. It was fair to assume that, with the money, the consumer could earn after taxes about the same rate of return as that paid on municipal bonds. (The interest on these bonds is essentially exempt from federal income tax.) However, beginning in 1988, the new tax law generally reduces everybody's top marginal income tax bracket to 33 percent. Consequently, in an October 1986 article, Consumer Reports states that, under the new Tax Reform Law of 1986, the shorter term mortgage may well become desirable for the vast majority of home buyers.

In conclusion, it's recommended that you first check to see if there are any tax savings for you under the current tax law in the 30-year loan. If not, or if you're in a gray area, you should give very serious consideration to a 15-year mortgage.

PREPAYMENT POLICIES

Lenders vary in their prepayment policies. Some assess no penalties; others limit the portion of a loan's balance that can be paid off early without penalty. In some states and on some types of loans, the terms of prepayment are a matter of law. For example, the laws in Massachusetts are particularly restrictive to the lender, while in California lenders cannot assess a prepayment penalty on most loans if the borrower refinances with the same institution.

Every mortgage contract should clearly specify the prevailing prepayment rules: the amount the institution will allow to prepay each year without penalty, the extent of the penalty if one is imposed, and the timing ofthe prepayments. Be certain that you understand the language and ramifications of the prepayment clause before agreeing to the terms of the mortgage.

The most common provision permits you to prepay up to one-fifth of the total loan each year. Anything above that is subject to a penalty.

How substantial are the potential savings? Consider the cost of borrowing money over a long period of time. With a 30-year mortgage at 12 percent interest, payments will add up as follows:

Loan Amount	Total Payments
$50,000	$185,151.60
60,000	222,181.20
70,000	259,210.80
80,000	296,244.00
90,000	333,273.60
100,000	370,303.20

The point is that over 30 years you pay for your house more than three times over! That's why it may be worth your while to practice mortgage acceleration.

How Mortgage Acceleration Works

Mortgage acceleration requires putting more money into monthly mortgage payments than you originally planned. For many families, this just isn't possible. However, even if you can manage extra payments only on a modest scale, you can get a worthwhile return. Here are some facts to keep in mind when you are thinking about mortgage acceleration:

1. The percentage of principal paid off in a 30-year loan by the twenty-fifth year is about one-half of the original amount borrowed. The remaining half of principal is paid off during the last five years. The exact portion varies with different interest rates:

Interest Rate	Percentage Paid Off by Twenty-fifth Year
8%	63.8%
9	61.2
10	58.7
11	56.2
12	53.8
13	51.4
14	49.1
15	46.9

2. An extra month's payment at the beginning of a 30-year mortgage can take an entire year off the time required to pay back the loan. Suppose you have a $50,000 mortgage at 13 percent with monthly payments of $533.10. If you pay $1,066.20 the first month (double your regular monthly payment), your loan will be paid in full in approximately 29 years.

3. A loan period can be cut in half if each monthly *principal* payment is doubled. In this case, a 30-year, $50,000 loan at 13 percent will be paid in full in 15 years and 1 month. Because you are increasing each month's payment to match the (increasing) amount of principal due as interest diminishes, payments start at $564.53, gradually rising to $1,083.39 at the end of the fifteenth year.

4. The same loan also can be paid in 15 years if you make equal monthly payments of $632.63.

5. It also can be paid in full in five years and three months if each month's payment is doubled from the required $553.10 to $1,066.20.

As stated before, it is assumed that it would be possible to prepay at that rate without penalty and that the homeowner can afford such payments. Doubling payments will cost you a total of $69,076.20, of which $19,076.20 is interest. Under the normal 30-year payment scheme, you will pay a total of $199,119.00, or $149,119.00 in interest. In other words, by doubling payments, you save an impressive $130,039.80 in interest and cut 25 years off the time required to pay off your mortgage.

Not every homeowner can afford the dramatic forms of mortgage acceleration discussed above. But every homeowner can devise a modified form of mortgage acceleration. As long as your loan is a standard, fully amortized mortgage, you can prepay your mortgage at your own discretion to the extent allowed under the terms of the contract, without penalty. You do not need permission to prepay; you simply mail more money than required. Today, many lenders include a space on the payment stub for such additional principal payments.

A small amount added to each month's payment has a substantial effect on the term of the loan and the total interest expense. Using as an example a 30-year, $50,000 mortgage at 13 percent interest, Table 2 shows payments without any acceleration; Table 3 illustrates the effect of an extra payment to the principal of $100 per month.

Table 13.2. FULL AMORTIZATION

Month	Payment	Interest	Principal	Balance
				$50,000.00
1	$553.10	$541.67	$11.43	49,988.57
2	553.10	541.54	11.56	49,977.01
3	553.10	541.42	11.68	49,965.33
4	553.10	541.29	11.81	49,953.52
5	553.10	541.16	11.94	49,941.58
6	553.10	541.03	12.07	49,929.51
7	553.10	540.90	12.20	49,917.31
8	553.10	540.77	12.33	49,904.98
9	553.10	540.64	12.46	49,892.52
10	553.10	540.50	12.60	49.879.92
11	553.10	540.37	12.73	49,867.19
12	553.10	540.23	12.87	49,854.32
Total	$6,637.20	$6,491.52	$145.68	

Table 13.3. AMORTIZATION WITH $100 EXTRA

Month	Payment	Interest	Principal	Balance
				$50,000.00
1	$653.10	$541.07	$111.43	49,888.57
2	653.10	540.46	112.64	49,775.93
3	653.10	539.24	113.86	49,662.07
4	653.10	538.01	115.09	49,546.98
5	653.10	536.76	116.34	49,430.64
6	653.10	535.50	117.60	49,313.04
7	653.10	534.22	118.88	49,194.16
8	653.10	532.94	120.16	49,074.00
9	653.10	531.64	121.46	48,952.54
10	653.10	530.32	122.78	48,829.76
11	653.10	528.99	124.11	48,705.65
12	653.10	527.64	125.46	48,580.19
Total	$7,837.20	$6,417.39	$1,419.81	

In other words, total interest was reduced by $74 and the total balance was reduced by $1,274 (interest saved plus the $100 per month) after only one year. Interest will be lower every month from this point on, since the outstanding balance is lower.

When an acceleration program is put into effect, the extra money paid against the mortgage balance is not spent. It's saved, and you pay off the cost of your house much more quickly.

ARMs and Mortgage Acceleration

So far we've only discussed mortgage acceleration programs aimed at fixed-rate mortgages. Acceleration programs, however, can also help holders of ARM contracts, sometimes to an even greater degree.

Acceleration can help avoid negative amortization (see Chapter 12), and can be started or stopped depending on the interest rate in effect.

Say, for example, you have an ARM mortgage that started at 9 percent. Over time, the rate moves up and down between 10 and 14 percent. The higher the rate, the more reason to make accelerated principal payments. The best strategy would be to increase the extra payments as the rate moves up.

When rates are low, you can decrease or stop accelerated payments. The money can be used instead for investments on which you might get a better return. Or you can continue your extra payments when rates are low and achieve an even more rapid amortization.

In short, mortgage acceleration can be a valuable tool for offsetting the effects of changing interest rates under an adjustable rate mortgage, especially if you feel secure enough to afford it. In any case, the homeowner should take the time to make careful comparisons of current investment opportunities before deciding to accelerate his mortgage payments. Depending on his or her tax bracket and the current financial climate, the homeowner may do better elsewhere.

S E C T I O N
III

INSURANCE

14

THE HOMEOWNER'S POLICY

In 1977, a fire swept through Santa Barbara, California, ravaging entire sections of this scenic West Coast community. The damage was immense and turned up a startling statistic: The average home destroyed by the blaze was covered by only one-half the amount of insurance required to replace everything that was lost. The reason: Property values in the area had soared, but the insurance policies of many residents had not been updated to reflect this good fortune.

Also, like many Americans, Santa Barbarans did not fully realize the value of what was in their homes. While it once was safe to assume that the contents of a home equaled one-fourth to one-half of the home's value, by 1977 that was no longer true. It is even less true today, as people continue to fill their homes with personal computers, VCRs, and other expensive electronic equipment.

According to the Insurance Information Institute, at least 8 out of every 10 homeowners carry too little insurance on their homes.

REQUIRED COVERAGE

A homeowner's policy consists of two broad types of insurance: liability and casualty protection. Liability is protection against your financial responsibility for injuries that occur to others on your property. If a visitor trips over a garden hose, slips on a slick sidewalk, or is injured in your pool and sues, liability insurance can protect you from a major loss. Casualty insurance, on the other hand, covers losses that you yourself suffer. The losses can be either man-made or from natural causes: fire, weather damage, vandalism, theft, etc.

You are required by the lender to have a homeowner's insurance policy for as long as you owe money on a mortgage. If you were not covered by this form of insurance and suffered a major loss, the lender may not be able to recover the loan. Once a house is paid off, you don't necessarily have to continue this insurance coverage, but you are taking a very big risk if you don't. A fire or other disaster could wipe out most of your equity in a matter of moments.

Some ill-advised homeowners have simply allowed their homeowner's policy to lapse; a 1985 survey by the Insurance Information Institute found that 4 percent of all American homeowners do not carry fire insurance and 3 percent said that they didn't really know whether they had any insurance at all.

The Institute also reports that homeowners lost $5.854 billion to fire-related losses in 1983, which is the most recent year for which we have such data. That year there were 523,500 fires in one- and two-family dwellings in this country. Extrapolating from this figure, it is reasonable to assume that if 4 percent of all homeowners do *not* carry insurance, more than 20,000 uninsured people will suffer devastating losses from fire each year. Homeowners may still own their land, but many will be forced to either rebuild their homes or move elsewhere and rent. That is not a pleasant prospect, but it does occur regularly.

While most homeowners do not let their home insurance policies lapse, many are not fully protected against a major loss. For whatever reason, they fail to increase the value of their coverage according to the replacement value of their homes and possessions. In this era of ever-increasing prices for single-family homes, that can be a very costly error.

UPDATING YOUR POLICY

Unfortunately, many homeowners tend to ignore their insurance policies. Insurance is not the most fascinating subject; it's a complicated and frustrating fact of life. Moreover, it's human nature to think "it won't happen to me."

How often a policy should be updated depends on a variety of circumstances, including:

1. Whether market values and construction costs in your area are changing

2. Whether the total value of your possessions has changed
3. Whether you've recently completed a major home improvement

There are policies that automatically increase the amount of coverage each year. The increase is based on the Consumer Price Index or on a state version of the CPI, depending on the insurance carrier. You will pay a higher premium for this kind of coverage.

You should also be aware that you may need additional insurance, since not everything is covered by a standard policy. For example, the standard policy will not cover business assets kept in your home or collections of art, rare coins, stamps, and the like. You also need extra coverage if you own expensive jewelry or furs.

The only way to find out if the total value of your assets is covered is to review your insurance policy carefully and regularly. Look at it several times each year to make sure you're fully insured. A regional vice president of the Insurance Information Institute put it this way: "The homeowner's policy should be considered a working document, to be reviewed every month or two. Keep it in the drawer with your monthly bills, and review it frequently."

How to Buy Insurance

The problem of underinsurance begins when you first buy a house. In the midst of all the red tape and deadlines of the closing, an insurance agent is hurriedly contacted and arranges coverage by telephone without even seeing your house. Sometimes the first year's premium is included as a closing cost. You automatically receive a premium notice each following year, or it simply will be tacked onto your monthly mortgage payment.

This is the worst possible way to buy insurance, because it initiates a casual attitude toward your policy. Instead, insist on finding your own agent, and ask him or her to see your home. Have him explain your various insurance options. Discuss in detail with the agent the amount of coverage you should carry as well as the different forms of insurance, inflation adjustments, and the advantages of various deductibles versus annual premium levels.

If an insurance agent is unwilling to make the trip to your new house, look elsewhere. Once you have a policy, a phone call to the agent is all that's required to increase coverage as your circumstances change.

When buying your first homeowner's policy, don't skimp on coverage to save a few dollars. It's a big mistake to pay a lower annual premium, and in the process forego insurance that you need. Cheaper policies often carry restrictions on what is actually covered, and you may be assuming more risks than you realize. Keep in mind, however, that not all insurance companies offer comparable service or rates. The price of a homeowner's policy varies not only from state to state but from neighborhood to neighborhood. It can vary with such factors as whether your house is made of brick or wood, how close you are to a fire hydrant, and how far you are from a paint factory.

Price is, however, an important buying criterion. Rates for the same coverage in the same location can vary by 50 to 100 percent, depending on the company you pick. It pays to shop carefully. First, decide what forms of insurance you need. Then ask for quotes from several insurance agents. Remember, homeowner's insurance is a fairly standardized product, with only a few versions available. So base your choice on price versus claims service, individual agent's service, and the company's financial stability.

HOW MUCH IS ENOUGH?

In order to know how much insurance you need, you must know how much your home and personal possessions are really worth. There are several ways in which this can be done.

For your home:

1. Hire a professional appraiser. The cost of such an appraisal varies widely, since it is not regulated in most states. An MAI (Member, Appraisal Institute)—an individual who has undergone a series of tests and has received an appraisal license—is considered to be the highest authority in the field. An MAI appraisal will probably be more expensive than one performed by an officer of a lending institution or an unlicensed appraiser, but if it determines the level and cost of your insurance, it's worth the extra expense.

2. Estimate what it will cost to replace your house. Replacement value is different from market value. *Market value* is what you can sell your house for today. *Replacement value* is what you will pay to have your house rebuilt, excluding the value of the land and the cost of the foundation. If you prefer to estimate the replacement cost yourself, measure the square footage of usable floor space in your house and multiply it by the current construction cost per square foot for homes of similar construction in your area. Your county

builders' association should be able to give you a cost-per-square-foot construction estimate.

3. Ask a local insurance agent. Someone who writes a lot of homeowner's insurance in the neighborhood will be able to tell you the approximate value of your house. But unless the agent is a qualified appraiser and actually comes to your home, it will only be an educated guess.

For your possessions:

1. Make an inventory of all your belongings. Keep the list in a safe place (such as a safe deposit box) for future reference. The total cost of your furniture, clothing, electronic equipment, and appliances is the lowest amount of coverage you should carry. Don't accept an insurance company's formula based arbitrarily on the amount of insurance coverage on your house.

2. Keep receipts for major purchases in the same safe place. Add these purchases to your inventory list and adjust your insurance coverage accordingly.

3. Make an inventory of any valuable jewelry, furs, and collections of art, rare stamps and coins, or other assets, and be prepared to verify the value of these items by keeping receipts and independent appraisals in the safe deposit box along with a clear, detailed photograph of each item.

However, on most insurance policies there are dollar limits for these types of high-value possessions. The limit is the most you'll get on the loss, no matter how many items are involved. To avoid losses on items with value exceeding the standard limits, you need to purchase an extra piece of insurance, called a *floater*. Floaters may be written as separate policies or as endorsements to a standard policy. The property to be insured must be "scheduled," that is, described in terms of quantity, quality, style, manufacturer, value, and so on. The estimated value must be supported by a professional appraiser's report or a bill of sale.

Floaters can cost from a few cents to a few dollars per $100 of coverage, depending on the item. Premiums vary with location and the crime rate of an area.

CUTTING COSTS

There are several ways to keep insurance costs to a minimum and still have the protection you need:

Accept a higher deductible. This means you must pay a certain amount of the loss before the insurance company pays the balance. By increasing your casualty deductible from $100 to $250, for example, you can substantially trim the annual cost of the policy.

Install security devices in your home, such as deadbolt locks and electronic security systems. These measures, besides giving you extra security, will get you a discount from some insurers.

Install fire and smoke detectors and alarms. These are mandatory in many states, especially in newly built homes and apartments. Again, many insurers will give a discount to homeowners with alarm systems.

Comparison shop. Compare rates for homeowner's insurance among three or four carriers, but be sure you're not comparing apples and oranges. Don't just look at the cost of the premium; make sure that coverage, limits and other provisions are comparable as well.

Consider purchasing one policy. In some cases, you can save money by combining different types of coverage in one policy. Insurance companies add a "load" to every policy in order to cover their general and administrative expenses plus the selling agent's commission. By combining homeowner's and auto insurance in one policy, for example, you may save 10 to 15 percent on the premium cost. This is partially a discount by the company, to get the additional business. Nevertheless, you should still comparison shop. Insurance companies that offer big premium discounts may be using inflated rates to begin with. It pays to check the rates of other companies that may not use such come-ons to determine which offers the truly favorable price for the coverage you need.

Another form of insurance—replacement-cost insurance—costs a little more but allows for increases in value. This is good coverage for both your home and its contents. However, some of these policies include limits, and so you still wouldn't recover the full replacement value of an item.

For example, such a policy may stipulate a limit of 400 percent times actual cash value. If you bought a home computer for $2,000, you won't necessarily recover what it would take to replace that particular model. If the "actual cash value" (replacement cost minus depreciation) was $300 when a loss occurred, the most you would recover would be $1,200 ($300 times 400 percent).

This coverage, while not ideal, is still better than an actual cash value policy, the traditional form of homeowner's insurance, which would allow you to recover only $300 for the loss of the computer.

15

LIABILITY PROTECTION

One of the major risks you assume in owning a home is liability. If someone is injured on your property, you can be sued or an insurance claim can be filed against you.

You can be held responsible not only for the immediate damages, such as the medical bills the injured person incurs, but for his or her time lost from work (which can be substantial) and the injured person's "pain and suffering" as well.

Some injuries to others can arise from incidents beyond your control. For example, if a rotten limb from your tree falls and hurts a passing pedestrian, you can be sued—simply because the tree was on your property. The fact that you didn't directly cause the injury doesn't matter. The complaint may charge that you should have known that there was a danger from that particular limb and you neglected to saw it off. You may be able to successfully defend the suit, or you may lose. Arguments are frequently made in liability cases that the homeowner could have prevented the accident in some way or another.

Here's another example: A neighbor's child is teasing your dog through the fence. The dog bites the child. Common sense says the child caused the accident, but in the world of liability, you are responsible for your pets' behavior and for any medical costs, pain, and suffering they may cause someone.

A judge can rule that an injured person and a property owner were both at fault to some degree. This is referred to as "comparative" negligence. The award will be based on a determined level of fault. For example, if a neighbor uses your ladder to climb on your roof without your permission in order to retrieve a ball, a rung on the ladder snaps and he falls, breaking his leg, who is at fault? The neighbor may blame you for leaving a dangerous ladder in an accessible spot. You will claim that he had no permission to be on your property at all. The judge may call this a case of comparative negligence.

Another form of partial fault is called "contributory" negligence. This occurs when someone sues for damages and, while you were at fault, the injured party was even more at fault. Your contributory negligence is minor compared with the other person's. Going back to the neighbor and the ladder, suppose it was at night and your neighbor had been drinking heavily. Furthermore, he had to go into your workshop to get the ladder. These additional circumstances shift the balance of fault significantly toward the neighbor.

WHAT IS COVERED?

Personal liability is a claim for damages resulting from your negligence. If you are not insured, your house can be taken away to satisfy a claim decided against you in court—not only your house but every other asset you own: your car, your business, and even your future earnings. In other words, a sizable lawsuit can wipe you out financially.

Homeowner's policies in recent years have offered a minimum of $25,000 coverage for liability for bodily injury and property damage. However, in our increasingly litigious society, many insurance companies insist on a minimum of $100,000, and sometimes more. For another $5 to $10 a year or so, you can have $300,000 of liability coverage, a slight extra cost well worth paying. (See the August 1985 issue of *Consumer Reports* magazine.) The more you have to lose, the more liability insurance you should carry.

A homeowner's liability policy should cover the following claims.

MEDICAL PAYMENTS. Medical bills can add up, even for small injuries. In many cases, an injury requires repeated visits to a physician, physical therapist, or hospital for a long period of time. Moreover, medical benefits are often paid to an injured person, regardless of who is at fault. Someone who through his or her own negligence is injured in your home or yard still can receive payments from your insurance company.

INJURIES AND PROPERTY DAMAGE. Someone can legitimately file a claim against you after suffering a loss while on your property, or because of some incident occurring on your land. This is true whether you or the vic-

tim is at fault or whether the accident is an act of God. For example, a limb from your maple tree falls, severely damaging your neighbor's roof. Or your 12-year-old child throws a rock through a neighbor's window. (This is classified as an "accident" until the child reaches the age of 13.) Perhaps a pesticide you're using in your yard drifts over to a neighbor's property, killing his outdoor ornamental goldfish or a prized shrub. Your liability insurance should cover all those possibilities.

LOSS OF EARNINGS. If someone is injured on your property and as a result cannot work, your policy covers his or her lost wages. Depending on the nature of the injury and the amount of time lost, this can be a large amount of money.

PAIN AND SUFFERING. This is the most difficult loss on which to place a monetary value, yet juries do so all the time. Their judgments can result in extremely high cash awards to the injured party.

WHAT ISN'T COVERED?

There are some forms of personal injury or property damage that are *not* covered under a homeowner's policy:

WORK-RELATED LOSSES. Homeowner's liability policies specifically exclude injury and damages that are work-related. Therefore, if you have clients, customers, or business associates working for you on your property, you will need additional protection.

You conduct a bookkeeping service from your home and a client comes by to drop off the books at the end of every month. On one such visit, she trips over your sprinkler and breaks her leg; later, she files a claim against you. In this case, because the nature of the visit was business-related, your standard liability policy will *not* cover you. For a small additional premium, you can obtain additional coverage or a separate policy.

Another example of how the business exclusion can work against you: If you have a garage sale and someone stops to look at your goods and is injured, you may or may not be covered; some insurance companies will apply different standards. If you hold garage sales regularly, it may be smart to stay on the safe side and get additional insurance. However, if you hold a garage sale only once or twice a year, you're probably covered under your standard homeowner's policy.

MALPRACTICE. The liability policies of professionals using their homes or an office on their property do not include malpractice insurance. This form of insurance must be obtained through separate coverage.

WORKING CHILDREN. Even though liability insurance covers you and your family, you can have a potential problem if your child does yard work or odd jobs for other people, or has a newspaper route. If in the course of that work your child ruins a flower bed or injures someone with his or her bicycle, you may not be covered.

Extra coverage is cheap. If your child has a regular job, a small annual premium can protect you from potentially large damage claims.

SECOND HOMES OR PROPERTIES. Your homeowner's policy will not cover liability on investment property. You must get separate coverage, as such property is considered a business for profit. You also need separate coverage for vacation homes.

AUTOMOBILES. Your homeowner's policy doesn't cover you for accidents in your car, boat, or plane. You must obtain other insurance.

DOMESTIC EMPLOYEES. If you hire a gardener, housekeeper, or regular baby-sitter, you probably need extra coverage. In some states, you're required to provide domestic workers with worker's compensation (a form of liability insurance for employees). Even if this is not required, an injury or accident involving a gardener or housekeeper can be denied by your insurance company.

INTENTIONAL DAMAGE. You are not covered for damages you do to your own property or injuries you intentionally inflict on others.

In summary, considering the infinite variety of situations in which a homeowner can be held liable and the low cost of liability protection, it is better to have too much than too little coverage. Every homeowner should carry the minimum $300,000 worth of liability insurance, and should consider carrying more.

Some people take out an "umbrella" liability policy that offers protection for many more risks that can occur around the house. This is extra coverage above and beyond the normal homeowner's policy. For the relatively small extra premium, you buy vastly more protection, including protection against claims arising from business activity, libel or slander suits, and other losses that most people don't usually worry about. This additional policy is

advisable for anyone who is wealthier than average, owns a very expensive home, or operates a business.

HOMESTEADING

Another way to protect your house is through the homestead exemption law.

A homestead is land that is occupied by the owner and his or her family. Most states allow for a homestead exemption, meaning that the owner of a home cannot be forced to sell his or her house or land to satisfy a claim for unsecured debts, including liability damages.

Homestead exemptions are allowed in every state except Connecticut, Delaware, the District of Columbia, Maryland, New Jersey, Pennsylvania, and Rhode Island. In some states, the exemption is automatic; in others, homeowners must apply, preferably when they purchase the property.

A declaration of homestead is filed with the county recorder, who is also the best source of information on the state's homestead regulations. You also may want to check with a real estate attorney. The amount of exemption is set by law, so the homestead exemption provides only limited protection. If, for example, your state allows a $40,000 exemption but you have home equity of $85,000, you can be forced to mortgage your home for the difference in order to pay a damage claim if you're not covered by your insurance. In a few states, the entire value of a property is covered by the homestead exemption.

To qualify for homestead exemptions, you must meet three criteria:

1. You must have a family. In a few states, a single person qualifies.
2. You and your family must live on the premises. This means you can have only one homestead exemption at a time.
3. You must own the property. In some states, a rental lease will qualify you.

Unsecured debts falling under the homestead exemption include not only possible lawsuits but credit card loans, for example. Not included in most states are property taxes or the amount owed on a mortgage or pledged under a lien.

16

CASUALTY PROTECTION

Every 45 seconds, a fire breaks out in a home in the United States. More than 7,500 lives are lost each year in these fires, and property damage totals nearly $6 billion annually. Fire is the most common casualty covered by homeowner's insurance.

Casualties are damages, losses, and accidents to one's home or belongings. While liability insurance protects you against losses and injuries to others, casualty insurance is designed to reimburse you for damage to your home and furnishings.

Fire insurance was the original type of casualty insurance. Compared with fires, other casualties account for only a minor portion of total insurance claims; hence, homeowner's insurance is often referred to as fire insurance. You pay substantial fire insurance premiums primarily because residential fire damage is so costly.

A fair percentage of fires in homes probably result from arson. Most fires, however, are accidental, caused by children playing with matches, smokers falling asleep in bed with lighted cigarettes, or flare-ups in the kitchen.

WHAT IS COVERED?

Eleven kinds of casualties are covered in every homeowner's policy and are referred to as the "11 common perils." You are covered for damages caused by:

1. Fire or lightning

2. Loss of property removed from the premises because of fire or other perils

3. Windstorm or hail

4. Explosion

5. Riots and other civil commotions

6. Aircraft

7. Vehicles

8. Smoke

9. Vandalism and malicious mischief

10. Theft

11. Breakage of glass which constitutes a part of the building

A policy that covers only these 11 perils is called an HO-1 policy. (The HO stands for homeowners.)

Seven additional forms of casualty are included in some policies:

12. Falling objects

13. Weight of ice or snow

14. Collapse of a building or any part thereof

15. Sudden and accidental tearing apart, cracking, burning, or bulging of a steam or hot water heating system or of appliances for heating water

16. Accidental discharge, leakage, or overflow of water or steam from within a plumbing, heating, or air-conditioning system or a domestic appliance

17. Freezing of plumbing, heating, and air-conditioning systems and domestic appliances

18. Sudden and accidental injury from electrical currents generated by appliances, devices, fixtures, and wiring (TV and radio tubes are not included)

A policy covering 18 perils is called an HO-2 or HO-4 policy (see next section for details).

Even more protection can be obtained in an "all risks" policy, which extends coverage to "all perils except flood, earthquake, war, nuclear accident, and others specified in your policy." This is an HO-3 or HO-5 policy.

Like liability insurance, casualty coverage is relatively inexpensive depending on size, location and construction of your house. However, the damage inflicted by these common (and uncommon) perils can be very costly to repair. A good rule of thumb for homeowners is, the more casualty insurance, the better.

There is an exception to this rule. Some forms of special casualty insurance are prohibitively expensive. In some areas hit by frequent floods or earthquakes, for example, premiums are so high that many homeowners simply can't afford the insurance. They must live with the danger, hoping for the best. When the worst does occur, it is common for the federal government and some state governments to grant low-interest loans to disaster-struck families for rebuilding.

POLICY TYPES

The common forms of casualty insurance include the following:

HO-1: THE BASIC POLICY. This provides less coverage than most homeowners need, only protecting your house and other possessions against the 11 common perils. No other losses are covered.

HO-2: THE BROAD FORM. Your dwelling and other possessions are protected against the 18 listed perils. This is more popular than HO-1.

HO-3: THE ALL-RISK FORM. The most widely used policy for homeowners, this includes the "all-other" clause, protecting your dwelling from all perils not specifically excluded in the policy. Your possessions are protected against only the 18 named perils, however.

HO-4: THE RENTER'S POLICY. This form of insurance protects renters' personal possessions, plus any improvements they may have made at their own expense, against the 18 named perils. The dwelling itself, of course, is not included.

HO-5: COMPREHENSIVE. This form covers everything on an "all-risk" basis except exclusions named in the policy. It is the most expensive form of casualty insurance.

HO-6: THE CONDOMINIUM AND CO-OP POLICY. This policy protects personal possessions and improvements. "All-risk" coverage is available. It can apply to condos as well as co-ops, since the word "condominium" is used by the insurance industry to mean both. It does not provide insurance for the dwelling itself, as this is normally carried by the condominium or co-op association.

HO-8: OLDER HOMES POLICY. This is similar to HO-1 in that it covers only the 11 common perils on a named basis. Some older homes contain fixtures and other materials that would be expensive to replace today. Under this policy, a damaged older home will be returned to serviceable condition, although not necessarily the same condition as before. It covers both dwelling and personal possessions.

COST AND INFLATION

When shopping for casualty insurance, be sure to compare costs for the *same* coverage.

Keep in mind that there are two ways in which the value of your home and personal possessions can be calculated for insurance purposes: according to actual cash value and replacement cost (see Chapter 14). You should expect replacement-cost insurance to cost 35 percent more. However, in the event of a large loss, it will be well worth it.

For even more money, you can buy a policy with an "inflation guard" provision. Most of these specify the percentage by which coverage will increase each year. However, expensive items, such as furs, jewelry, and stamp and coin collections, are not included in the inflation provision. You can buy additional coverage at an additional cost. You might do better to get separate insurance policies for these precious items.

LIMITS IN COVERAGE

There are limits in the standard casualty insurance policy, all of which must be listed in the contract for insurance. Most common among these are:

$500 to $1000 maximum on:
- Stamp collections, passports, securities, and manuscripts
- Boats, their motors, and furnishings
- Trailers
- Jewelry, furs, and precious stones

$100 to $200 maximum on:
- Money, precious metals, and coins

$1,000 to $2,500 maximum on:
- Silverware and silver-plated or gold-plated ware
- Firearms

17

WHAT DO YOU OWN?

The benefit of drawing up a complete inventory of one's possessions and keeping it up to date cannot be stressed enough. In the event of a loss, this could be your only tangible proof of ownership.

A household inventory should include four types of information:

1. The article and a description of it
2. Purchase date
3. Purchase price
4. Its location in your home

The description of an article should be as specific as possible. For example, avoid vague descriptions such as "home computer system." "IBM PC computer with 128K disk drive" is much more precise.

This goes for furniture as well. Rather than simply describing an item as a "couch," be more elaborate: "couch—six feet long, leather-upholstered, bought new from Jones Furniture."

The purchase date is important, too, even if it is only an estimate. It helps establish an item's depreciated value at any given date. If you aren't sure about the exact age of your belongings, the insurance company may assume that they are older than they really are and pay you less for their loss or replacement.

Purchase price is the key to value. Be as exact as possible. If you have sales receipts, look up the amount you paid and record it in your inventory report. Avoid estimates, if possible.

For this reason, hold on to sales receipts, especially for major purchases. They will help verify claims. If you own furniture or stereo equipment that is more expensive than the average purchase, your insurance company may prefer to set a replacement value lower than the item's actual cost to you. A sales receipt would be the final word.

A well-organized inventory report keeps each room and its contents listed separately. This makes it easier to add new inventory later and will also help to avoid duplication. Moreover, in the event that damage is limited to one part of your home, you will know precisely what is lost.

WHERE TO KEEP THE INVENTORY LIST

You will defeat the purpose of compiling this important information if you keep the master inventory list at home. In the event of a fire, for example, all your records can be destroyed along with your possessions. Make copies of the inventory and send the original to your insurance agent for his or her files. Put another copy in a safe deposit box. These security boxes can be rented at any bank or savings institution at a reasonable fee, depending on the size of the box. Or leave a copy of your inventory with a trusted friend or relative.

Since many families now own their own video equipment, another way of recording inventory is to put it on film. It doesn't take much time and the film easily can be stored in a safe place. The advantage of video is that it constitutes virtually undeniable proof that you own what you claim. Remember to update the tape from time to time, just as you would a written inventory.

If you don't have a video camera, you can also photograph every room. Include views of each wall, and be sure to capture clearly all of your major possessions. Again, keep the photos in a safe place.

Don't overlook anything when you compile your inventory list. Include the paintings on the wall, the valuable contents of drawers, even the carpets under your feet. They will all have to be replaced in the event of a major fire or other disaster.

18

MORTGAGE INSURANCE

You've probably seen the advertisements on TV: The setting sun is filtering through the windows of a grief-stricken family's home. One parent has died, and the family now stands to lose its home, since it will no longer be able to afford the monthly mortgage payments. Things look hopeless for these people, but a reassuring figure appears on screen, saying, "This doesn't have to happen to you." And it won't happen, he goes on to say, if you and your family are protected by such and such an insurance policy.

What *will* happen if you or your spouse dies suddenly or is unable to work? Will you lose your house? Mortgage insurance is designed to protect you and the lender from the financial consequences of your death or disability.

IS THERE A NEED?

There's no reason to buy insurance that you don't need. If you have a tremendous net worth or two incomes that are both adequate to make house payments, you don't need the extra coverage. Of course, only a minority of homeowners fit this description.

Many people misunderstand the meaning of mortgage insurance. The name implies that it is a form of protection for your mortgage. It's not. The term is used to refer to a form of either life or disability insurance on you, with the amount of protection pegged to the balance you owe on your home, or on the mortgage payments you are required to make monthly. When you buy life insurance directly (as opposed to mortgage insurance) you compare premium rates and other factors for various levels of coverage. How much protection you buy is up to you, with the cost based on your age and general health. However, with mortgage life insurance, the amount you get is tied directly to the outstanding balance on your mortgage. If you die, the insurance company will pay off the mortgage for your family.

The same is true with disability insurance. If you buy a nonmortgage disability policy, you decide how much coverage you need in order to pay living expenses if you are disabled, and you pay a premium based on your age and occupation. If you become disabled, the insurance company will give you a certain amount of money each month to cover these expenses. But a mortgage disability policy specifically covers your mortgage payments if you're unable to work.

If you already have adequate life or disability insurance, you may not need extra mortgage insurance. In addition to any individual policies you may own, you may receive life or disability insurance as a fringe benefit on the job. Many employers provide a certain amount of life and disability coverage based on one's annual salary.

To decide whether you do need extra insurance, look at the total amount you now carry. Compare this with your current sources of income. If you die or become disabled, can your family continue to make mortgage payments without your income? If not, you need extra insurance.

There are two ways to go about getting additional protection. You can take out a mortgage insurance policy, or you can buy a policy not tied to your mortgage. The second course is usually preferable, since a mortgage is only one of the expenses your family would have to cope with if you died or became disabled. In fact, mortgage insurance should never take the place of adequate life insurance coverage for your family.

MORTGAGE LIFE

Mortgage life insurance is a form of decreasing-term insurance, meaning that the premium cost stays level throughout the contract but the amount of benefit declines each year. The term—the period of insurance—is the length of time it will take to pay off the mortgage on your home.

The less you owe on your mortgage, the less of a bargain mortgage life insurance becomes. Therefore, you should keep a few points in mind.

If you practice any form of mortgage acceleration, you may pay off your mortgage more quickly but will still be paying for your insurance coverage as though you were paying only the required amount each month.

There comes a point at which it is cheaper to cancel the mortgage life policy and replace it with a nonmortgage form of insurance. This point can be determined only by comparing rates on other insurance with what you're paying currently for your mortgage life insurance policy.

It pays to consider how mortgage acceleration can affect your mortgage insurance. If you are making extra payments to the principal of $100 a month, the amount of mortgage insurance in force is lowered accordingly, since mortgage life coverage always equals the amount of debt on your mortgage. In other words, you have increasingly less coverage, but your cost is just as high.

When is mortgage life no longer a bargain? Here's an example. Assume that your insurance payments are $42 a month, your mortgage balance is $60,000, and you're 30 years old. In 25 years (without any accelerated payment of your mortgage), you'll owe about $30,000 on your mortgage, but the amount outstanding will be declining rapidly. However, your mortgage life payments still will be $42 per month.

At this point in your life, what would you pay for a five-year decreasing-term life insurance policy for $30,000? The answer depends on several factors, such as your age, health, and occupation. If you can get the same amount of coverage for less than $42 per month, it's time to switch over.

When to Drop the Coverage

Assuming you buy mortgage insurance at all, the time may come when it makes sense to discontinue the coverage. Consider the situation we described above.

You will have built equity in your home of more than half the balance even without taking into account the house's appreciated value.

You probably will have accumulated other assets and may not need the protection.

With only five years to go on the mortgage term, your family may not have a hard time paying off the mortgage on the house in the event of your death.

Your children most likely have grown up and left home, taking pressure off your household budget.

If you have more than one mortgage, the question of whether to carry insurance becomes more complicated. You'll need separate policies for each mortgage. In almost all cases, you'll be better off buying a life insurance policy to cover *all* your debts. By combining your coverage, you save some money in premiums and also reduce the number of payments you're required to make.

As stated previously, another benefit of having a life insurance policy not tied to your mortgage is that, if you die, your family has a choice of what to do with the death benefit. With mortgage insurance, the loan balance is paid off, period. There are times, though, when your family will do better to continue making mortgage payments and use the insurance money for other expenses. For example, if interest rates rise but your mortgage rate is fixed and is relatively low, your family can invest the insurance proceeds at the current high rate and continue making the monthly mortgage payments.

Lenders are usually the major promoters of mortgage life insurance. Many of these insurance policies are sold to homeowners through advertisements sent in monthly mortgage bills or mailed separately from an affiliate of the lender. (Sometimes the ad looks like an invoice, and some homeowners pay the bill automatically, assuming that it's money they owe the lender.)

You may be paying for mortgage insurance without even knowing it. If you are paying impounds with your monthly mortgage payment, chances are that they include property taxes and perhaps homeowner's insurance premiums. They may also include payments for mortgage insurance.

Some mortgage contracts require that you pay mortgage insurance premiums as long as your equity in the house (percentage of the appreciated value of the property) is below a specified level. You have no choice. This in effect is a form of default insurance for the lender, virtually eliminating the lender's risks in the event of your disability or death. Once your equity exceeds the specified level, you have the right to cancel the mortgage insurance. But some lenders make this cancellation extremely difficult, refusing to drop coverage unless you can prove that your equity exceeds their limit. Lenders have been known to charge a homeowner for an independent appraisal and later refuse to let the owner see the results, simply informing him or her that the equity is insufficient to justify dropping the insurance.

If the lender refuses to cancel your mortgage insurance and you see no reason to carry it, hire an appraiser on your own. Presenting the current valuation of the house to the lender should result in removal of the premium from your monthly payment. If the lender refuses, complain to the proper regulatory body (depending on the lender's charter, either a federal or state bureau). Advice also is available from the American Council of Life Insurance (call the hot-line number: 800-423-8000).

To protect yourself, be sure that you're always aware of what is included in your monthly mortgage payment. Get copies of all insurance policies for which you are paying premiums. Also, check directly with the insurance company periodically to ascertain if the insurance is still in force; some lenders, through negligence or design, continue to collect premiums for mortgage insurance even after the coverage has expired.

JOINT MORTGAGE LIFE INSURANCE

One variation on mortgage life is called joint life mortgage insurance. If making monthly mortgage payments depends on your having two incomes, joint life affords especially good protection. For a single premium, it covers both spouses. If either one dies, the entire mortgage balance is paid off.

Premiums will be higher than for a conventional policy, since the insurance company is taking a risk on two lives rather than one. Some factors affecting the cost of a joint mortgage life policy include the ages of the husband and wife, the outstanding balance on the mortgage, and the number of years until the mortgage will be paid in full.

This form of insurance tends to cost less compared with carrying two separate life insurance policies, because there is almost always a savings in combining policies. But, again, mortgage insurance is not a good replacement for an adequate life insurance policy.

The provisions of a joint mortgage life policy are the same as those for a single mortgage life insurance policy. Premiums remain level through the term of coverage, but the amount of insurance declines as the mortgage gradually is paid off. One big difference is that it may not be as feasible to replace one policy with another, even when cheaper rates are available, since the crossover point is more complex, with two lives involved. If either spouse has a health problem, for example, it may be impossible or too costly to get a replacement policy.

MORTGAGE DISABILITY INSURANCE

Disability insurance is a form of coverage that pays a specified monthly benefit if you become disabled and are unable to work for a long time or permanently.

What counts as being disabled? That might seem a simple question, but upon examination it becomes complex. Is the person able to do any work at all? Has he or she suffered a loss of income? And if so, how much? These are some of the elements that go into a definition of disability.

Every disability income policy contains its own definition. And it is the policy's written definition alone—not paraphrasing by a salesperson—that determines what benefits will or won't be paid. You should insist on seeing a sample policy before purchase. Read it carefully, with a special eye to the way disability is defined. Some policies consider you disabled only if you are unable to do *all* the duties of your regular job, not just the main duties. Ideally, the policy should state that you're disabled if your income goes down as a result of sickness or an accident. Since income loss is what you're insuring against, a pure income-loss test of whether you're disabled makes the most sense. (See the March 1983 issue of *Consumer Reports* magazine.)

Insurance agents refer to disability as a form of "economic death," or loss of earning power, which in many ways is more devastating to a family than the death of its breadwinner. This is especially true if the family has all the life insurance it needs but has no protection whatever against disability.

Disability involves a loss of income as well as the possibility of high medical bills that often are not covered by health insurance policies. All too frequently unprotected disability results in the loss of a home, other assets, and even personal bankruptcy.

Often people who purchase this form of insurance coverage fail to update it periodically. An accident occurs, and they discover that their disability insurance cannot make up for an income that has increased considerably over the years. Disability insurance, like all forms of insurance, must be reviewed and updated regularly.

Whether you select a mortgage disability policy, or one that is not connected to your mortgage, or you are covered under an employer's group plan, make sure that you have enough disability protection to offset a loss of income. You need to replace only your after-tax income, since the benefits from a disability policy are not taxed. In many cases, Social Security disability benefits can help pay for part of the load. A good disability insurance agent can explain these benefits and coordinate them with a disability policy.

19

MONEY-SAVING INSURANCE TIPS

If you're like the average American consumer, your insurance needs are numerous—when you look at the total cost of covering yourself and your family against every possible loss, you probably wish you were in the insurance business. However, there *are* ways to reduce costs. Here are some tips:

LIFE INSURANCE. Do not buy a whole-life policy. Buy the amount you need in the form of term coverage. This will save a lot on premiums.

LIABILITY AND CASUALTY. Always carry the amount you need. Don't skimp. Take into consideration the replacement cost of items, not the original price. Premium costs can be cut substantially if you take on a larger deductible. You'll have to pay for minor claims, but that is the risk you take—the savings in annual premiums usually makes it worthwhile.

DISABILITY. Every disability policy specifies a waiting period before benefits begin. Thirty days is common, though it is possible to get very expensive coverage that starts immediately upon your suffering a total disability. If you can survive a 30-day or even a 60-day waiting period, you can reduce your cost.

HEALTH. As with liability and casualty insurance, you can increase the deductible amount on your policy and cut your premium costs. The same caveat applies: Are you in a position to pay for minor illnesses or injuries?

Combining two or more policies may be the best way to cut insurance costs and still carry all the protection you need. When you combine risks, you get several other advantages. It's simpler to make a single payment on

one policy than to pay several companies. In addition, reviews of your overall insurance coverage are easier, and you're more likely to update one form
of protection when you review your policy for another.

The major disadvantage of combination policies is that you aren't
shopping for the cheapest and/or best of each type of insurance. You also
have less flexibility to change coverage in the middle of a policy year without giving up some of your savings, and you often end up stuck with coverage you no longer need just to keep good rates in effect.

One likely combination—the most common—is homeowner's (liability
and casualty) plus auto (also liability and casualty) coverage. Because coverage is so similar, a combination policy may be cheaper, depending on the
carrier. If you have both homeowner's and auto coverage with one carrier,
your agent can tell you the difference a combined policy would make.

If your homeowner's insurance is included as part of your monthly
mortgage payment, this is not an insurmountable problem. The impounded
payment often goes to a subsidiary of the lender, and so naturally the lender
may resist any attempt to replace this insurance with a policy from another
carrier. However, you have the right to cancel this insurance whenever you
want, even if your contract requires you to have some kind of homeowner's
insurance. Simply provide the lender with proof of your new insurance policy; your agent can supply this.

Another comparison worth undertaking is the cost of separate insurance policies for two different cars and the cost of a combination policy.
Depending on the state in which you live, either form may be cheaper. It
also depends on the individual driving records of you and your spouse and
your company's policies on assessing premium increases and allowing lower
rates for safe drivers, among other things. If one spouse has a perfect driving
record while the other has a poor one, for example, separate coverage may
be the best way to go.

IMPROVEMENTS

20

FINDING A
CONTRACTOR

Not too long ago, when an American family outgrew its living quarters, or wanted added features in a home, the solution was quite simple—move. Today, trading up is a luxury that not too many families can afford. Improvements and expansions are often less costly than moving, and so most homeowners opt to stay where they are and renovate and remodel rather than relocate.

As a result, the home improvement business is booming. According to the U.S. Department of Commerce, American homeowners spend between $46 and $60 billion annually to maintain, improve, and remodel their homes, and the figure is rising. Like any successful business, the home improvement industry has its share of frauds. According to state contractor boards, homeowners most often report the following three complaints.

1. Contractors' poor business practice. For example, the money you pay the contractor may go to paying suppliers, subcontractors, and other employees for work done on a previous job. Thus payments to them for doing your work often depend on future contracts—if none are immediately forthcoming, it can mean long delays in completing your job even if you've paid for it in full. Or the contractor simply takes on too much work in fear of not getting enough, and cannot do your work on time.

2. Incompetent work. Sometimes a contractor fails to adequately supervise his or her employees and the work just isn't up to par. Or the person you hire doesn't have the experience or expertise to complete the job adequately.

3. Scams. These fly-by-nights are every homeowner's night-mare. For example, you make a large down payment for the work, only to discover that the contractor has disappeared with the money.

FINDING THE RIGHT PROFESSIONAL

A contractor is not necessarily the person who actually does the phys-ical work on your home. Frequently the contractor acts as a coordinator of the project, hiring subcontractors to do the actual construction work.

Try to find a qualified professional by checking other sources.

OTHER CUSTOMERS. Any contractor you choose should come highly rec-ommended. Ask for references. If a contractor is unable or unwilling to fur-nish these, go elsewhere. Anyone who has happy and satisfied customers will gladly give you their names and numbers. Don't settle for photographs. Visit the homes of these customers and carefully examine the contractor's work. Ask the customers if they are satisfied with the quality of the work, the con-tractor's professionalism, and inquire about the length of time it took to complete the job.

NEIGHBORS, FRIENDS, AND RELATIVES. Do you know anyone who re-cently had work done on his or her property? If you do, take a look at the work and, if impressed, ask for referrals. The chances of finding a good con-tractor this way are better than if the contractor contacted you on his own.

SUBCONTRACTORS. Most contractors hire subcontractors to do special-ized work: plumbing, electrical work, painting. Some subcontractors are good sources of referrals and will readily give you the names of highly respected contractors in the area. But this is not foolproof—the subcontractor may not tell you the entire truth, especially if he or she is dependent upon the con-tractor for delayed payments or future jobs.

STATE LICENSING BOARD. Most states license contractors. Check with your state board to make sure that the contractor you're considering is cur-rently licensed and in good standing. Don't accept as proof the fact that a contractor is able to produce a state license number. Check to make sure that it's current. Be sure the license is for the type of work you want done, since most states give out different licenses for different types of contractors. (See supplement at the end of this chapter for further information and addresses of state licensing boards.)

LOCAL BUSINESS GROUPS. The Better Business Bureau can help identify contractors who have clean records, but if there have been complaints to the BBB about a particular contractor, the group will not usually give you the specifics of each case.

The Chamber of Commerce can refer you to its own members who are contractors, but is not likely to tell you if complaints against any of them are on record.

A local chapter of the National Association of Homebuilders (NAHB) can refer you to the right type of contractor and local chapters such as Remodeler's Councils can refer you to a qualified member.

The NAHB is a national trade association with 750 local affiliates and a total membership of more than 125,000 contractors. For more information, contact the NAHB's Remodeling and Rehabilitation Department, 15th and M Streets, Washington DC 20005. Or phone: 202-822-0200.

OTHER CONTRACTORS. If you know a contractor but he or she does not do the kind of work you need done, that person can still refer you to other reliable contractors. In fact, a professional contractor is likely to be one of your best sources of referrals.

Whatever the source, get as many names as possible, at the least three. Look for names that come up again and again. Anyone who does quality work for a fair price will be recommended repeatedly.

ESTIMATES AND PLANS

For comparatively simple jobs, such as a basic bathroom remodeling, a hand-sketched plan will do. While preparing an estimate, a contractor frequently will draw up a preliminary description of what you want done. Make a copy for yourself, being sure to jot down all the specifics you've discussed with the contractor. Then, when you get an estimate from another contractor, you'll have something with which to compare it.

For more complex projects, a professionally prepared set of plans and specifications should be drawn up. The extra cost of preparing such plans and specs will save money and avoid misunderstandings in the long run. Your contractor will hire a draftsman, designer, or architect to draw up the plans, with your approval. They will lay out exactly what is to be done, and the specific dimensions involved. Specifications will include a detailed list of the type, size, and quality of materials to be used.

You should get at least three estimates. If one of the three estimates is extremely low, the contractor probably is underbidding on purpose to get the job but probably won't deliver the same quality in craftsmen or materials.

An unusually high estimate may mean that you're being given an estimate with more in it than you asked for. If all three are wide apart, it may mean that you changed the description of the job when you spoke with each contractor. That is a common mistake made by homeowners seeking estimates. The first contractor to give you an estimate may make suggestions, some of which you will accept. By the time you get to the third estimate, your idea of the job will be more all-inclusive than it was when you started out. The estimates then will vary widely, since actually they will be for very different jobs.

To avoid this problem, describe the job in as much detail as possible, and include drawings whenever possible. If you agree to any of the contractor's suggestions, write them down and incorporate them in your job description. When you get to subsequent contractors, give them the same modified job description or, if you change your mind, let the first contractor submit a revised bid. Then you can be sure that you are being quoted prices for the same job.

BUILDING PERMITS

Once you select a contractor, sign a contract (see Chapter 21), and draw up plans, the next step is to obtain all the licenses and building permits that are required. Every city and county has a different set of rules for regulating construction or large-scale improvements in a private home. These codes fall under the state powers governing health and safety requirements.

You can obtain licenses and permits on your own or the contractor will do it for you. Many people prefer to let the contractor handle these arrangements. If the contractor does agree to get the needed licenses and permits, make sure you receive copies. In most areas, the actual permit must be posted at the job site and periodic inspections and approvals must be conducted, including a final clearance of the entire job.

If you fail to go through the required licensing and permit procedures before construction begins, you may be in for expensive trouble. A building inspector can force you to tear down or redo the entire project. Be sure you're aware of local regulations governing home improvements before you hire a contractor. If the individual contractor you hire says that it's not necessary for the local building inspector to know about the job, don't believe him. You'll be better off working with a professional who stays within the law.

You should be present whenever a building inspector comes to check out the work. That is the time to ask questions. If there are problems, you should know exactly what they are, and make sure that they will be corrected to the inspector's satisfaction, and to yours. Such problems could involve the use of shoddy or substandard construction materials, inadequate or poorly designed waste disposal units (such as septic tanks), or insufficient and hazardous electrical installations.

Without periodic inspections, you will have no way of knowing whether the contractor is following local standards for safety and quality. Don't fall for the argument that the contractor will save you a lot of money by avoiding these inspections; it is rare for a building permit to cost more than $100 to $200, and the protection it gives you is worth it.

ZONING

Another important matter to consider before you begin any large-scale improvement or construction in your home is the zoning regulations in your neighborhood. If your building plans do not meet the local zoning restrictions you will have to go for a variance, or a variation on the zoning laws. This entails submitting an application to the local planning board, paying a fee, and waiting for a hearing to be scheduled. Your neighbors will receive a registered letter informing them of your application and giving them the opportunity to attend the hearing and register their dissent or approval. Be warned: getting a variance is often no easy matter, especially if your building plans directly affect a neighbor's view or significantly change a neighborhood's appearance. Neighborly opposition can be fierce and, in many communities, dissension over zoning infringements has led to bitter and protracted disputes. If possible, try to get some idea of the local feelings about your proposed improvement and be prepared to meet any criticism with substantial data on how your project will or will not affect your neighbors' properties. Needless to say, a calm and reasonable manner on your part will most likely assist your case.

OTHER THINGS TO BEWARE OF

Avoid trouble by following these additional rules:

1. Watch out for door-to-door solicitation: Be especially careful of those who offer to perform work on your home for you. A true professional gets business from referrals and perhaps advertising but rarely by hiring salespeople and soliciting

homeowners directly. Some companies promise referral fees for using your home as a model. The fees rarely materialize, and the practice is illegal in many states. A large number of these door-to-door selling operations are not from legitimate contractors but rather are scams in which the company takes large deposits from homeowners and then leaves town without doing the work. Moreover, the offer to look your house over for contract work can be a way of casing the house for a burglary.

2. Know what you're signing: Don't sign anything until you've read it thoroughly. In some cases, an estimate can be worded in such a way that your signature makes it a binding contract. Avoid this by not signing any estimates. If a contractor insists that you sign anything before you are ready to do so or you're not sure exactly what it is you'll be signing, consult with an attorney before putting your name on any document.

3. Keep a file: Be as well organized as you can, making sure that everything is agreed to in writing and that you receive all the necessary documentation. Everything—estimates, permits and licenses, contracts, and change of work notices—should be organized and kept in an accessible file.

SETTING A PAYMENT SCHEDULE

Always make sure that your agreement with a contractor includes a specific payment schedule. This should be in writing and stated as clearly as possible.

You should rarely, if ever, agree to make an advance payment except when it is to be used for identified out-of-pocket costs. These costs include deposits on building materials required by suppliers, licenses, and any payments to a draftsman or architect that must be made before the work begins.

Payments to contractors should never exceed the amount of work that has been completed to that point. If you pay in advance, you have no leverage if trouble or delays develop. As long as you withhold a portion of the full payment large enough to cover the completion of a job at any point, you will be protected. Then, if the contractor for any reason fails to complete his or her end of the contract, you will still be able to afford to hire another contractor to finish the job.

This practice also protects you against the problem that some contractors experience with their money management. By getting behind in their payments to subcontractors and suppliers, they end up using payments on one job to pay their debts on a previous one. As the problem escalates, they go deeper into the hole. Eventually, they are so far in debt that every customer and every job is put in jeopardy.

STATE LICENSING BOARDS

To make sure a contractor's license is valid and that the person is in good standing, check with the board in your state that is responsible for licensing and regulating contractors. Some states require licenses only for certain types of work or for work above a specified contract amount. Be sure to ask for the criteria when you write or call. Following is a list of state boards that enforce requirements for residential work:

State Licensing Board for General Contractors
125 South Ripley
Montgomery, Alabama 36130

Division of Occupational Licensing
Department of Commerce
P.O. Box D
Juneau, Alaska 99811

Registrar of Contractors
1818 West Adams Street
Phoenix, Arizona 85007

Contractors Licensing Board
621 East Capitol Avenue
Little Rock, Arkansas 72202

Contractors State License Board
3132 Bradshaw Road
Sacramento, California 95827

Business License Division
820 French Street, 10th Floor
Wilmington, Delaware 19801

Board of Construction Industry
111 East Coastline Drive
Jacksonville, Florida 32202

Contractors License Board
P.O. Box 3469
Honolulu, Hawaii 96801

State Licensing Board for Contractors
7434 Perkins Road
Baton Rouge, Louisiana 70808

Retail Sales Tax Division
License Bureau, Room 404
301 West Preston Street
Baltimore, Maryland 21201

State Board of Public Contractors
637 North President Street
Jackson, Mississippi 39205

Department of Commerce
Public Contractors
1424 9th Avenue
Helena, Montana 59620

State Contractors Board
70 Linden Street
Reno, Nevada 89502

Construction Industries Division
Regulation and Licensing Department
Bataan Memorial Building
Santa Fe, New Mexico 87503

Contractors Licensing Board
7509 Hayworth Drive
Raleigh, North Carolina 27609

Secretary of State
State Capital
Bismarck, North Dakota 58505

Department of Commerce, Builders Board
Labor and Industries Building, Room 403
Salem, Oregon 97310

Residential Home Builders Commission
2221 Devine Street, Suite 530
Columbia, South Carolina 29205

Board of Licensing Contractors
1808 West End Building, 4th Floor
Nashville, Tennessee 37219

Division of Contractors
P.O. Box 45802
Salt Lake City, Utah 84145

State Registration Board of Contractors
3600 West Broad Street
Richmond, Virginia 23230

Department of Labor and Industries
Contractor Registration Section
P.O. Box 9689
Olympia, Washington 98504

21

THE HOME IMPROVEMENT CONTRACT

No matter how large or small the job, or how much faith you have in the integrity and honesty of a building contractor, a written contract is an absolute necessity for your protection.

Professional contractors will comply with this rule as a matter of practice. If you are considering a contractor who is unwilling to give you a written contract but instead proposes to do the work based on a verbal agreement, look for someone else.

WHAT SHOULD THE CONTRACT INCLUDE?

Every contract for home improvements should include several basic provisions, such as the following.

NAMES AND ADDRESSES. The contractor, his or her address, and the address where work will be performed should be written into the contract. If your state has licensing, the contractor's state license number should be included as well.

DESCRIPTION OF WORK. The work to be performed should be described in enough detail so that it is clear exactly what is expected from the contractor. This should include a full description of materials to be used and a list of any appliances or equipment that are a part of the deal.

DATES. Contracts should include the start and completion dates of the work. These dates should be spelled out precisely.

TWENTY-DAY NOTICE. A clause stating that a failure to begin work within 20 days of the specified beginning date is a violation of the contract may protect you against unnecessary delay.

COST AND PAYMENT SCHEDULE. The total cost of the job should be specified, along with a payment schedule based on the completion of the work. Payments should be staged as described in the previous chapter, so that you pay for work as it is completed, not in advance. Generally, a good payment plan is 15% at the beginning with another 15% to be paid when the work is completed. The remaining balance is staggered at intervals in between, or as the situation warrants.

PERMITS AND LICENSES. There should be a list of the licenses and permits needed and an indication of who will be responsible for obtaining them.

THREE-DAY CANCELLATION NOTICE. There must be a clause stating that you have three days in which to cancel the contract.

NOTICE TO OWNER. A brief description of your state's lien laws should be included. Its importance is discussed later in this chapter.

OWNER'S RIGHTS AND RESPONSIBILITIES. A contract should describe your contractual duties and rights, chiefly related in this case to the payment schedule.

WARRANTIES. All warranties of materials or workmanship that the contractor is providing should be described in full.

REMOVAL OF MATERIALS. Look for a statement that ensures that the contractor will clean up and remove all material and debris from the job site when the work is completed.

CONTRACTOR LIABILITIES. Make sure there is a statement that the contractor is responsible for worker's compensation and other liability insurance for his or her workers, suppliers, and subcontractors. If a workman has an accident while working on your property, and the contractor does not have insurance, you could be sued for any damages.

CHANGES IN WORK. This provision allows the owner to request changes in writing without invalidating the entire contract.

WORK STOPPAGE. The contractor will insist on the right to suspend work on the project if you fail to make payments.

COMPLETION BOND. This is an agreement that the contractor will supply a bond ensuring completion of the work. In other words, if the contractor fails to complete the project, an insurance company will pay for the balance to be done. Including this in the contract will cost you 2 to 5 percent extra, but it's worth having.

IMPORTANT NOTICES

The two most important provisions in every home improvement contract are the three-day cancellation notice and the notice to the owner. These commonly are included with the contract, as separate forms. Another important document is the unconditional lien release which the contractor gives you at the completion of the job.

THREE-DAY CANCELLATION NOTICE. Also called the notice of right of recission, this is a form advising you that you have three days to cancel the agreement from the date of signing a contract for home improvements.

If you change your mind, you sign the notice and send it to the contractor via registered mail, with return receipt requested.

The notice includes language such as the following:

> Notice to Customer Required By Federal Law: You have entered into a transaction on (date) which may result in a lien, mortgage, or other security interest on your home. You have a legal right under federal law to cancel this transaction, if you desire to do so, without any penalty or obligation within three business days from the above date, or any other date on which all material disclosures required under the Truth in Lending Act have been given to you. If you so cancel this transaction, any lien, mortgage, or other security interest on your home arising from this transaction is automatically void. You are also entitled to receive a refund of any down payment or other consideration if you cancel. (The notice goes on to specify the date by which you must notify the contractor or lender of your decision to cancel.)

NOTICE TO OWNER. This document is not signed but should be given to you when you enter a contract. It explains your state's lien laws. Several disclosures may be included. Commonly, the language reads like this:

Under the Mechanics' Lien Law, any contractor, subcontractor, laborer, supplier, or other person who helps to improve your property but is not paid for his work or supplies, has a right to enforce a claim against your property. This means that, after a court hearing, your property could be sold by a court officer and the proceeds of the sale used to satisfy the indebtedness. This can happen even if you have paid your contractor in full, if the subcontractor, laborer or supplier remains unpaid.

The notice may also disclose the name and address of the state contractor's licensing and regulatory board and the requirement that a contractor's current license number be included in the contract.

UNCONDITIONAL LIEN RELEASE. This form is signed by the contractor at the completion of the job and, in some states, notarized as well. The important language is the waiver itself, which reads something like this:

The undersigned hereby expressly waives and releases any and all mechanic's lien rights, stop notice rights, notice to withhold rights and bond rights and all and any claims whatsoever against the property hereinabove described.

This form should be sent after the final payment of your bill to the contractor. By giving you this release, the contractor protects you in the event he or she fails to pay his suppliers or subcontractors. Without such a release, those creditors can place a lien on your house (or building, in the case of a co-op or condominium), forcing you perhaps to pay double for a job or, in extreme cases, making it imperative for you to sell your home in order to satisfy the lien.

COVERING YOUR LIABILITIES

Since you can be required to pay for work done twice over, an unconditional release is a good safeguard. As an additional safety measure, you should receive lien releases from all subcontractors and suppliers as the job progresses and their part in the job is completed. In fact, before making the periodic payments to the main contractor, be sure you have received lien releases from any subcontractors, such as the plumber or electrician, as soon as their involvement in that phase of the work is over. By the time the job is completed, make sure you have received *all* releases you need to ensure that everyone on the job has been fully paid.

Once work starts you will probably receive a preliminary lien notice from each subcontractor or supplier. This is *not* a filed lien, merely the preliminary step required in the event that the subcontractor is not paid and a lien is later filed. Be sure that all the final releases match all the preliminary notices you were sent at the beginning of the work.

As mentioned previously, you have some risk whenever a contractor or a working crew of subcontractors, laborers, or suppliers is on your property. Make sure that your contractor has a current worker's compensation policy as well as business liability insurance. This insurance clause should be clearly stated in the contract and you should insist on seeing proof of such insurance coverage.

You may also safeguard against liability to workers in your house by your taking out additional insurance. You pay an extra premium for coverage for one year only (the minimum term that insurance companies usually will insist on) so that any injuries to workers are sure to be covered. Be certain that this added liability protection covers not only the contractor but the contractor's employees, subcontractors, and suppliers as well.

If the improvement will add to the value of the house, be sure to increase your homeowner's insurance coverage accordingly. Begin the increased coverage from the initial day of construction. In this way, you are protected if materials are damaged before the job is completed.

As a final step, you can request as part of your contract that a Notice of Completion be filed with your county upon completion of work. This is a recorded statement identifying the property, the contractor, and the owners. It then states that "A work of improvement on the property herein described was completed on (date)."

In some areas, the contractor is required to file this notice; in others, the owner must. Even if you are not required to file this notice, it is a good idea to do so or to make sure that the contractor files it for you.

The value of a Notice of Completion is that it ensures that your liability is at an end. There is a waiting period following completion of a project, after which liens cannot be filed. The Notice of Completion advises anyone involved with the project that the waiting period, usually 30 days, has begun. Thus, if your contractor fails to pay a subcontractor for work performed and the waiting period expires, the lien probably will not be valid (although there are exceptions to this rule). Without a recorded Notice of Completion, the actual completion date is not clearly identified.

OTHER CONTRACT TIPS

If your contracted work is under way and you decide that you want additional improvements, be sure to complete a *written change order*, signed by both parties. This necessary procedure should be explained in your contract and set up in such a way that the original contract is not voided by your additional request.

The change order should specify the cost of the extra work as well as any revision to the scheduled completion date, if necessary.

There are a few things you should *never* do when under contract for a home improvement.

DON'T SIGN ANYTHING YOU DON'T UNDERSTAND. Get a full explanation of anything you sign and have an attorney review it if you have any doubts.

DON'T ENTER INTO SEPARATE AGREEMENTS. Don't agree to anything with subcontractors or suppliers without clearing it first with your contractor.

DON'T PAY CASH WITHOUT A RECEIPT. It's always preferable to pay by check. However, if you must pay in cash, be sure to get a signed receipt stating the amount you've paid and what it was for.

22

ACTING AS YOUR OWN CONTRACTOR

You don't have to hire a contractor if you would rather coordinate and supervise the work yourself. As your own contractor, you can save quite a lot of money by avoiding the general contractor's markups. However, unless you have construction experience, big jobs are best left to the experts.

If you have no experience in plumbing, for instance remodeling a bath or kitchen can be a complicated job. You may end up needing a contractor anyway, entailing delaying the job while you search for one and perhaps spending more money for materials than you'd originally planned. This applies to any specialized work: masonry, roofing, electrical work, installing a floor or exterior wall, or even installing Sheetrock.

Do-it-yourself home remodeling and improvement is a big business. A large portion of the homeowning public has ventured into this market, only to find that many jobs are far more complex in the doing than they originally appeared on paper.

THE DANGERS

There's no point hiring a contractor for small maintenance jobs. Most people can figure out how to put on their own weather stripping, paint a room, or install a door handle. But if you're adding a room, replacing a roof, or installing a swimming pool, you had better be an experienced and skilled handyman or be prepared to work with a contractor.

The primary reason anyone begins a home improvement on his or her own is to save money. The savings *can* be substantial, but first you must decide whether they're worth the risks. Consider the special pitfalls that await the do-it-yourself contractor:

INEXPERIENCE COSTS MONEY. Unless you're versatile and skilled in the many steps involved in a major home improvement, you can have no idea of what you're up against. You also won't have an accurate idea of what the project will eventually cost. At the worst, you could be left with a financial disaster and an unfinished job. Doing work incorrectly also means more expense and further delays.

IT TAKES MORE TIME. Assuming that you have a regular full-time job, the work will have to wait for weekends and evenings. Unless you can take off from work, a job that takes a general contractor two weeks to complete can take you two months or more. This means more dust, noise, and inconvenience for your family.

EVERYTHING IS UP TO YOU. You not only need to complete the work on your own, but you also must negotiate bids with any subcontractors you hire, draft and sign contracts, arrange financing, prepare plans, get permits, and schedule the job from beginning to end.

FINANCING IS MORE DIFFICULT. Many lenders refuse outright to lend money for do-it-yourself improvements, since their risks are much higher.

YOUR LIFE IS DISRUPTED. Your life can be turned upside down by a big job, making you wish you'd hired a contractor and paid the extra money in the first place. The added stress on your family can also make the experience far less rewarding than you may have thought at the outset.

COORDINATING SUBCONTRACTORS

When you act as your own general contractor, you can farm out the entire job to subcontractors and never have to lift a finger for the actual construction. But, even if you go to that extreme, you're still responsible for supervision and scheduling, which are the most critical parts of the job.

When you hire your own subcontractors, it's best to exercise the same level of care that you use when you hire a general contractor. This process must be repeated for every subcontractor you hire. With a major renovation, this can mean as many as 15 specialists. Even if you have only six—

plumber, electrician, carpenter, floor installer, painter, and Sheetrock company—it can be a formidable job. You still must prepare and sign contracts, set a schedule, coordinate inspections, and so on.

As an example, you're remodeling a bathroom—not expanding it, only replacing the existing fixtures and relocating pipes, installing a new floor and an additional window, and painting the entire room. Assuming that plans have been approved, all bids have been received, and contracts with subcontractors have been signed and assuming that you have ordered all the new fixtures you'll need and have been given a firm delivery date (keep your fingers crossed), you can begin to set up a schedule.

Because you're not certain how much time to allow for each phase, you want to be generous, so you estimate that the job will take about a month. A general contractor probably can complete this work in one to two weeks, but you're not sure, so you allow more time.

You plan to tear out the old fixtures and the existing wall and floor over a weekend. No problem—that is, until you discover that you don't have the right tools to detach sink, toilet, and bathtub connections. Not only that, you discover that you don't know how to stop the flow of water. Then you realize that you can't haul away the ancient bathtub all by yourself.

Is this your only bathroom? If so, your family has a problem. Will you move into a hotel for a month or stay with a cranky relative? Or can you schedule the job tightly enough to complete everything so the facilities will be out of order for only a few days? You're not sure, and so you pad the timetable even more.

Then a subcontractor arrives, and you learn that he or she doesn't have the right parts or equipment to complete the task. Now you'll have to reschedule everything from that point forward.

You can see that from the start of the job there is an abundance of potential problems.

YOUR EXTRA LIABILITY

Even if the job proceeds like clockwork, you have another risk: increased liability.

What if someone on the job gets hurt? This is a risk you take even when working through a general contractor, but the contractor's experience and knowledge make such accidents less likely to happen. If a subcontractor is injured because you did some preliminary work incorrectly and created a hazard, you may well be liable for damages. For example, you tear up your old floor and fail to warn a subcontractor. The subcontractor walks into the room and falls through, breaking an arm. Or you stack materials carelessly and a heavy appliance topples over, seriously injuring a worker.

Remember, you're the general contractor. If you hire a subcontractor, negotiating a fee for work to be done under contract, check to make sure the subcontractor carries his or her own liability and worker's compensation insurance. If you hire a worker for daily wages, you are required to provide worker's compensation and to withhold social security, federal tax, and state tax. If you don't, you may be required to pay the taxes for your employee later. Example: You hire a laborer to help tear out an old porcelain tub and you pay him in cash to avoid all the paperwork. He later claims to have pulled a muscle in his back and files for a partial disability. But you didn't have worker's compensation. You're in big trouble.

What happens if there are cost overruns? You'll have no one to blame but yourself, and you'll have to find the extra money somewhere.

Some examples:

When you first estimate the bathroom renovation, you overlook the cost of tile, a new medicine chest, and mirror. These add up to over $1,000, but you've already used all the money from your home improvement loan. The subcontractors are ready to do their part in the project but have no available materials to install.

Or, when the plumber begins to install your new pipes, he finds a connection that has rusted through, so a new length of pipe must be installed. You must find some way to pay for the extra material and labor costs. When you work with a general contractor, you agree in advance to an exact cost for labor and materials and have the legal means to ensure that you won't have to pay a penny more.

If neighbors are injured or their property is damaged because you have extensive work underway, you can be sued: You leave old fixtures in your backyard and a neighbor's child wanders in, falls over your old sink and suffers a concussion. While you are removing the old bathtub from your yard, it drops and cracks your neighbor's adjoining driveway. These incidents may seem uncommon, but similar ones happen every day.

A Checklist for Do-It-Yourself Improvements

If you decide to be your own general contractor, follow these steps to prevent the most common pitfalls of the do-it-yourself project:

PLAN AHEAD. Do as much research as you can. Find out what materials cost and shop around for prices. Also find out about the cost of delivery of materials and the time required from order date to actual delivery.

CHECK WITH THE LENDER. Find out if your lender is willing to carry a loan for a project you will manage yourself. Be sure to line up financing on the best possible terms before contracting with anyone.

CHECK SUBCONTRACTOR REFERENCES. Go through the same reviewing steps for every subcontractor you hire as for a general contractor. Ask for references, check state licenses, and get a written estimate before signing any contracts. Get enough estimates so you can make a proper decision.

DRAW PLANS AND SPECIFICATIONS. A general contractor can work from partial drawings and explain to the crew exactly what should be done, but anyone who acts as his or her own contractor cannot afford to leave any details to chance. Have plans drawn up by a professional architect, along with a detailed material specifications list.

GET REQUIRED PERMITS. Be sure to check with the local town planning department about what local permits and inspections are required. Obtain permits before you start work and be sure to schedule time for the building inspections.

DRAW UP A JOB SCHEDULE. Plan every phase of your job. Consult with subcontractors to determine how much time will be required and allow time at every step in case anything goes wrong.

CHECK INSURANCE RISKS. Make sure you're completely covered in case any liabilities arise. A professional subcontractor should have insurance, but check your added risks as well.

SUPERVISE. Spend time at the job site and supervise your subcontractors. Make sure that arrival dates are honored and that suppliers deliver what you need according to promised schedules.

ALLOW FOR INCONVENIENCES. Think ahead about disruption of your normal family life. You'll have strangers in your house, open walls, dust, and noise the entire time work is in progress. If you'll be without a bathroom or kitchen for any length of time, you'll probably have to move out until the job is nearly complete. Plan ahead for all of these problems.

SCHEDULE PAYMENTS WITH WORK. Don't prepay subcontractors. Final payment should be made only after completion, inspection, and approval by you and your building inspector.

CHECK SUBCONTRACTORS' SUPPLIERS. Just because you're your own contractor, you're not protected from a mechanic's lien. Check directly with your subcontractors' suppliers to make sure they have been paid.

23

FINANCING AN IMPROVEMENT

This is a true story: One homeowner wanted to add a den to his house. He looked into the cost of drawing up plans, getting local permits and building materials, and the cost of hiring subcontractors for foundation, electrical, and plaster work. He took his facts and figures to a lender and got a home improvement loan for $12,000.

After getting well into the job, however, he discovered that it was a lot harder than he'd thought to build floors and walls and to stay within the budget on materials. The job was also taking more time than the owner ever imagined. He ran out of money and tried to borrow more, but the lender could not advance more funds, since she was bound by the institution's policy limiting loans to 80 percent of a home's value. The job was never finished. On top of everything else, the hapless owner lost his job and eventually the house.

The lender also was faced with a dilemma. Here was a house she had been forced to foreclose on, with an unfinished improvement for which she had already advanced money. In order to recapture this investment, it was necessary for the lender to pay out even more money in order to finish what had been started. In the end it proved impossible to make up the total cost of all the loan and construction funds.

Experiences like this make many lenders very cautious about funding major, expensive home additions or renovations especially when the owner does the contracting.

If you're contemplating such an undertaking, the likelihood that you'll be able to locate financing for your home improvement will depend on three major factors:

1. The amount of equity you have in your home

2. Your credit history and current level of income
3. The type of improvement and whether you'll do the work yourself or through a contractor

The equity you've built up is critical to the lender, who wants to make sure you have enough of a share in the value of the property to guarantee that the loan will be paid back.

When you first buy, most lenders require that you personally hold a 20 percent interest in your house. They will finance the balance of 80 percent. If your new house is valued at $90,000, a lender will probably finance up to $72,000. The balance of $18,000 must be covered by your down payment or by a combination of cash and a second mortgage, if the lender allows.

When you undertake an improvement, the same rules may apply, but with a slightly different formula. For example, if you are planning a $20,000 improvement to your $90,000 home, this will raise its value to $110,000. A lender may finance 80 percent of that total, or up to $88,000. Subtracting the balance of your mortgage from the $88,000, you arrive at the maximum amount a lender will finance—$19,000.

Value of house with improvement	$110,000
80%	88,000
Minus outstanding mortgage balance	69,000
Maximum financing available	19,000

This rule won't always be that simple to apply. The lender may discount the maximum market value of your home in some cases. If the lender believes that a $20,000 improvement will add only $15,000 to the value of your home, the formula will be adjusted:

Value of home with improvement	$105,000
80%	84,000
Minus outstanding mortgage balance	69,000
Maximum financing available	15,000

However, it is tough to get a lender's agreement to carry a home improvement loan at all if you plan to do the work yourself, no matter how high your equity. If you're an experienced craftsman who has done home improvements in the past, furnish the lender with proof of your competence. Take photographs of the improvements you've done for yourself or others, and present them to the lender along with reference letters from your satisfied homeowners.

The question of adequately estimating the cost of the work to be done is an important one for the lender. If your estimate turns out to be too low and you run out of money, the lender is stuck with an unfinished job and an insolvent homeowner. If, on the other hand, a hired contractor gives you an acceptable bid that is stated in the contract, he or she is bound to complete the agreed-on work for that fee. This is a very powerful argument from the lender's point of view for only financing home improvements supervised by professional contractors and not novice do-it-yourselfers.

FINDING THE RIGHT FINANCING

Whether you do your own work or hire a contractor, there are several sources of financing available:

CASH. If you have the money, fine. You can save thousands of dollars that you would otherwise pay in interest on a loan. But don't deplete your everyday emergency funds in the process; always be sure to keep some money on hand where you can get at it quickly.

INSURANCE POLICIES. If you have a whole-life insurance policy, you may have built up cash value over the years. You can take out a low-interest policy loan to pay for the home improvement.

CREDIT UNION. This is another possible source for moderate- or low-interest loans. If you belong to a credit union at work, find out how much you can borrow and at what interest rate.

CONTRACTORS. It may be possible for a contractor to obtain competitive rates from a lender for the job. However, because the lender will make payments directly to the contractor, you don't have the same control as you do when you get your own loan. With your own loan, you can withhold payment on each phase of the job until the work is completed.

FINANCE COMPANIES. You can get a home improvement loan from a finance company, but you will pay top interest rates in most cases.

SAVINGS AND LOAN ASSOCIATIONS. The savings institution is a popular source for home improvement loans. Many will finance a first mortgage up to 30 years, but they will limit home improvement loans to 15-year terms or less.

BANKS. Terms vary from one bank to another. Many will finance purchases of homes or refinancing but don't want to touch home improvement loans. Others actively seek the business by offering competitive rates.

THE FEDERAL GOVERNMENT. Government loans are available for improvements to your home at competitive or low rates, but often with restrictions. There may be a ceiling on the amount you can borrow or a limitation on the purpose of the loan. For example, an FHA improvement loan insured by the Department of Housing and Urban Development must be used only to improve your living space. You cannot apply for such a loan to add a swimming pool, greenhouse, or new fixtures.

If you live in a rural area, you can apply for a Farmers Home Administration loan. However, your income level must fall within certain guidelines set by the FmHA.

STATE GOVERNMENTS. Most states offer home improvement loans at below-market interest rates, usually with restrictions on use or area, in addition to ceilings on homeowners' incomes. Call your State Mortgage Financing Agency or Housing Finance Agency for further details.

EQUITY LINE OF CREDIT. A bank, savings institution, brokerage house, or other lender will sometimes allow you a line of credit that you can use in any way you'd like. There are special dangers to this form of financing, which is discussed below.

PRIVATE SOURCES. You can borrow money from a private investor, a relative, or a friend or arrange a second mortgage through a mortgage company. Terms may be as short as 3 to 5 years or as long as 15 years. Rates may be higher than those available from other lenders.

A LINE OF CREDIT

Your home is a valuable asset, and bankers know it. Today, many of the country's banks, savings and loan associations, and even brokerage companies are offering homeowners a new "service": a line of credit based on the amount of equity you have in your home.

You probably have seen the TV ads advising you to "put your equity to work" and "use the money lying idle in the investment of your home." You tend to feel naive and non-enterprising if you don't take advantage of this great opportunity. But that's silly—when you pledge your home equity as collateral for a loan, you are simply borrowing money that will have to be paid back eventually.

A traditional mortgage allows you a fixed amount of money to purchase a home, but with an equity line of credit the lender allows you to borrow up to a specified amount, regardless of how much you really need. If you have $50,000 equity in your home and the lender will give you 80 percent, you have an equity credit line of $40,000—even if you need only $10,000.

This kind of credit line turns your home equity into a type of charge account—you are supplied with free checks that you can use freely. Many of these programs allow you to pay interest only—to a point. Once you reach a specified level of indebtedness, you must begin to pay off the loan.

This form of credit is seductive: it's all too convenient, too easy, to slide gently and painlessly into debt. Over time, all the equity in your home can be eroded through compound interest charges. For example, if you had a line of credit for $100,000, assume that you did the following:

1/1/87	You borrowed $22,500 for a home improvement.
4/1/87	$11,200 was spent on a new car.
7/8/87	$6,600 went to consolidate other debts.
9/1/87	You used $8,300 for a family vacation.

If you're paying interest only, how much will you owe after one year? A total of $48,600 has been borrowed, but only $22,500—less than half—was reinvested in the house. Meanwhile, your payments are up to $567 per month for interest only, which is quite a burden on the monthly budget for many homeowners.

At some point in the future, most likely between 5 and 10 years, the whole loan will come due. At that time, many unfortunate homeowners are forced to sell their homes or refinance the debt. You may find yourself wondering how you ended up owing so much money. A new car usually is replaced in a few years and adds nothing to your home equity. Consolidation of debt is a poor use of the line of credit, as you are likely to have those debts back at their original level within a year. A vacation financed with such a loan may be fun at the time, but merely an insubstantial memory when the time comes to pay back the loan. Another dangerous aspect of home equity loans is that many of them carry floating interest rates. If the rate soars, you could be thrown into extreme financial difficulty.

The equity-based line of credit is designed by lending companies that hope to realize great profits from the accumulating interest due on these loans. After all, the lender runs virtually no risk; the loan is guaranteed by the lien placed on your house. You, however, can lose everything. For most homeowners, the equity line of credit is a source of funding that should be avoided completely or used with great discretion.

THE DANGERS OF OVER-IMPROVING

If you're improving your home mainly for your own enjoyment and comfort, that's one thing. If, however, you're remodeling in order to add

...... value to your home, perhaps in anticipation of a sale in a few years, you should become aware of the dangers in over-improving on your original investment.

A neighborhood generally has a price ceiling to its homes. If a three-bedroom, two-bath house in your area sells for $80,000 to $95,000 tops (based on sales during the last year or two), there's absolutely no investment value in improving the house much beyond that price level. If your house is valued at $90,000, adding a den, swimming pool, and family room won't increase its actual market value very much. Your total construction costs can add up to $45,000, but that doesn't mean that your house will sell for $135,000. A house's value is always set more by neighborhood and general location than by the amount of money and care you put into it.

Some improvements have their own built-in limitations. A swimming pool, for example, can actually inhibit a sale. Many families with small children see it as a danger, while others don't want the extra cost of insurance and upkeep that comes with it. Or they may prefer the extra yard space, and thus cross your home off their list of serious prospects. Similarly, greenhouses, elaborate landscaping, or solar power systems do not appeal to the average home buyer and may make your home simply more difficult to sell.

In general, remodeled kitchens and bathrooms are the improvements most likely to add immediate resale value to your house. These are the most lived-in areas of a home, and up-to-date facilities in these rooms appeal to every home buyer. The addition of a second bath is another good investment with an immediate return for your money.

REFINANCING YOUR HOME

You can refinance your home in order to pay for a large-scale home improvement, but before you do, consider these points:

1. Don't refinance if your first mortgage or mortgages are at rates lower than current interest rates.

2. Be sure that you can afford the payments and that you understand the terms of the new loan. For example, with rare exceptions, you should not give up a fixed-rate loan for a variable-rate one. Lenders carrying an older loan at a below-market rate will make an offer that seems attractive in order to motivate you to make such a move, but you're always better off with a lower-rate, fixed-rate mortgage loan.

3. Be prepared to pay a prepayment penalty if you're paying off an older mortgage. This is worthwhile if you're getting a

break on interest rates. Even then, it may take a few years to break even on what you'll pay in penalties.

4. If your new consolidated loan includes cash to finance a home improvement, be sure the amount is sufficient. Remember, you'll need money for the closing costs involved in the refinancing: points, credit report, prepayment penalty, and so on.

5. You can reduce interest by taking out a separate loan just for the improvement and paying it off over a shorter period of time. The sooner you pay off a loan, the lower your total interest costs.

ENERGY CONSIDERATIONS

You also can save money by keeping in mind how much a possible home improvement will cost you in future energy bills. A new living room with an unusually high ceiling may be an elegant touch, but in later years, when heating and cooling bills may have increased, it will lose much of its appeal.

Beware of other energy-inefficient improvements that in the long run will cost you even more money, including:

- Too many windows. Windows are poor insulation at any time of year. If they face south or west, they will catch the hottest sunlight. If they face north, they tend to let in the cold.
- Skylights and sliding doors. These must be placed carefully and must be of high-quality materials to be energy-efficient.
- Open spaces. A large room with no separations or dividers takes longer to heat and cool.

An improvement can also have unexpected effects on the rest of your home.

For example, one family expanded their house, doubling the size of their family room and adding a new dining room. In the process, they removed a wall separating the kitchen from the original family room. Within a year, they realized that they had built in several expensive features. The family area, twice its original size, was difficult to heat and cool. In warmer months, the heat from cooking in the kitchen warmed up the rest of the house; previously the wall had isolated the oven heat. In cooler weather, a new sliding door and windows made for poor insulation and drafts throughout the main floor. In fact, their heating and cooling bills were so much higher that they ended up rebuilding the wall separating the kitchen from the family and dining areas.

Another family remodeled their bathroom and in the process covered the room's only window and replaced it with a vent. The vent did keep heat and moisture to a minimum, but in summer the owners had been accustomed to leaving the window open in the evening, allowing a cool breeze to waft through their bedrooms. Without the window, these rooms tended to stay unbearably hot, so air conditioners had to be installed. The moral of the story: Even a small renovation, undertaken without sufficient study, can add to energy costs and make your living space less comfortable.

24

THE STRESS FACTOR

Perhaps the most ignored aspect of a major home improvement is the accompanying worry and stress that invariably comes with the experience. "It isn't unusual to see a newly remodeled home go up for sale shortly after the work is completed," says one remodeling contractor. "The couple gets the work finished and then files for divorce. The improvement doesn't cause the problem—it just brings it right to the surface."

A major project certainly doesn't always lead to divorce, but if you have never lived through one, consider all the problems you'll face:

- Strangers will be coming and going all day long, making your house about as private and peaceful as Grand Central Station.
- Constant noise will interrupt normal routines.
- Dust will settle everywhere: in your bathroom, bedroom, and kitchen and even on your food.
- If you won't always be at home, the contractor may install a lockbox; strangers will have access to your home.
- You won't be able to walk into parts of your own home while the work is going on.

The problem is intensified when you're acting as your own contractor. Then you have the worst of both situations. Not only are suppliers, inspectors, and subcontractors wandering in and out, you're also under tremendous pressure to complete the job on time and within the budget.

DEALING WITH THE STRESS

There's not much you can do about the inevitable strain, but you can do several things to at least minimize the problem:

MOVE OUT. Trying to adjust to the routines of daily life with accompanying loss of privacy and living space is difficult if not impossible. You're often better off taking your family out of that hectic environment, even if it means an expensive hotel bill, especially if the work will take more than a few days.

KEEP YOUR TEMPER. One general contractor advises restraint between owner and contractor at the job site—no displays of temper in front of your family and the crew since it's unlikely that either of you will back down from such a public confrontation. Get away from everyone and discuss and resolve your problems with the contractor in private.

ARBITRATE SERIOUS CONTRACT DISPUTES. What can you do if you and the contractor cannot agree on the intent of a contract clause? It may be necessary to go into arbitration—you should get a fair price, and the contractor should be allowed to earn a decent profit. Your lender or an attorney can help locate an arbitrator.

PLAN WELL IN ADVANCE. "The more planning you do up front, the less will go wrong," a remodeling contractor advises. That means detailed plans, precise agreement on a payment schedule, inspections and approvals, and a work schedule your family can live with.

DELINEATE RESPONSIBILITY. Be sure that everyone involved understands where his or her job begins and ends. If you're working with an architect, a designer, and a general contractor, be sure that the lines of responsibility are clearly drawn. The job can only be more complicated and delayed if these professionals run into a conflict.

To avoid this problem, hire architects or designers recommended by a trusted contractor. If these professionals have worked together before, your project is more likely to run smoothly and be completed on time.

You will also avoid unnecessary stress if you use common sense and do the following:

- Inspect the work thoroughly, but once you're satisfied, make agreed-on payments promptly.
- Stay out of the contractor's way and let him do the job.
- Keep children and pets well away from the workers.
- If you have questions or objections, wait until the contractor has a free moment and discuss the issues quietly, away from the work site.

- Don't pester the contractor with constant change orders; if you do have changes, give them to the contractor early in the job.
- Honor appointments consistently, keeping in mind that contractors have scheduling problems just like everyone else.
- Remember that your contractor has a family and a private life, just as you do; don't bother the contractor excessively at home.

SECTION
V

TAXES

25

KEEPING TRACK OF YOUR INVESTMENT

Owning a home means keeping records—quite a few of them, and for a long period of time.

When it comes to a question of storing all the paperwork, a good rule of thumb is: if in doubt, keep it. It's advisable to create one large file and place all the records and documents pertaining to your property in it. This single file can be used for every type of form or record you acquire, whether at the point of sale, or later when improvements are made in the house. This housing file will become larger than any other file you keep and it will continue to grow as long as you own your home. Of course, vital documents such as the deed to your property or the proprietary lease and certificate of shares to your co-op or condo should be kept in a safe deposit box for maximum safety. These boxes can be found at most banks and the fees are currently tax-deductible.

You will need these records primarily for tax purposes and for when you sell your house—the IRS advises that you keep all tax documents for a particular year for at least three years after filing the return.

Records establishing the cost and basis of your home—purchase price plus or minus adjustments—will have to be kept for as long as you live in your house. When you sell it, you must retain all records for at least three years beyond that year's deadline for filing tax. Because a new home's basis is dependent on the adjustments you carry over from your previous home, you also must retain the original documents for as long as you're in the second home. In short, keep all these records for as long as you're a homeowner.

You can simplify your record keeping to some degree. For example, most mortgage companies supply you with a stub for each monthly payment that usually shows the total payment, the due date, and the amount applied to principal, interest, and impounds (the amounts withheld to pay insurance or taxes). At the end of each year, an annual summary is sent to you, showing the total amounts paid in each category. Once you receive the annual summary, throw away the monthly stubs.

If you replace one homeowner's insurance policy with another, the older one can be discarded. Upon completion of a home improvement, destroy unaccepted or unneeded estimates, minor correspondence and other miscellaneous paperwork that does not establish your adjusted basis or satisfaction of your debt to the contractor.

The following is a list of the typical documents every homeowner will accumulate over the years, divided into three categories: ownership, insurance and mortgages, and improvements.

OWNERSHIP RECORDS

LEGAL DESCRIPTION OF PROPERTY. A document that tells precisely where the property is located and its dimensions. Typically, the document gives the property's location—county or city—along with degrees and measurements representing your property's boundaries, and also pinpoints it on a map.

CLOSING STATEMENT. This is a summary of the total price of the property, including prorated taxes, insurance, and rents, as well as other closing costs.

DEED OF TRUST OR MORTGAGE. This is a document by which you transfer rights to your property to the lender until the debt is totally satisfied.

LOAN DISCLOSURE STATEMENT. The lender's summary of the amount you are borrowing, the interest rate and the APR (annual interest rate) as required under the Federal Truth In Lending Act. The total of all payments, the starting date for payments, and the amount due each month are included in this statement.

PROMISSORY NOTE. This is a document signed by the buyer acknowledging the mortgage debt.

TITLE COMPANY'S PRELIMINARY REPORT. This is a summary of the title search performed a few weeks before the actual closing.

TITLE INSURANCE POLICY. The policy issued on completion of the final title search. It pays you, or the lender, or both, should your title prove invalid.

DEPOSIT RECEIPT. This is the document signed by buyer and seller at the point the offer is accepted, including all terms and contingencies.

PEST CONTROL INSPECTION REPORT. This report is issued by a pest control company to determine the extent of pest damage if any and indicate the degree of repairs necessary.

OTHER INSPECTION REPORTS. The reports of home inspection services or contractors, including a description of defects and repairs that should be made, are also necessary to keep on file.

WARRANTIES. This refers to any documents—in printed form or letters from real estate brokers or prior owners—ensuring the condition of your property and any of its components.

INSURANCE AND MORTGAGE RECORDS

FIRE INSURANCE POLICY. This is the policy that is currently in effect insuring you against property liabilities and casualties.

MORTGAGE INSURANCE POLICIES. These are policies insuring that your family, in the event of your death or disability, will be able to pay off the mortgage on the home.

PROPERTY TAX STATEMENTS. These statements are mailed to you from the county assessor's office, breaking down the semiannual or annual tax bill on your property and showing due dates for payment.

Your property tax bills usually are paid directly to the tax office by the lender (bank), who collects a set amount of money each month from you through an impound. This is an additional amount you pay along with your monthly mortgage loan payment. You can request that the impounds be stopped. In that case, you will be responsible for paying property taxes directly to your county tax assessor's office, usually twice a year, in a lump sum. Many people prefer including the payment monthly to the bank rather than having to come up with such large amounts of money twice a year.

MORTGAGE PAYMENT STATEMENTS. These monthly stubs show your payment date, amounts applied to principal, interest, and remaining balance due. They can be discarded on receipt of the annual summary statement.

RECONVEYANCE NOTICE. This is a copy of the notice filed at the county records office upon full satisfaction of a debt on your home, including all mortgages.

ASSESSMENT AND IMPROVEMENT NOTICES. These are notices by local authorities of planned improvements (for new sewers or water mains, sidewalks, or curbs, for example). These are commonly one-time costs or increases in the assessed valuation of your property.

AREA ASSESSOR'S MAP. This is a copy of the page from your county's book of maps showing the property divisions in your neighborhood. It will be supplied free of charge when assessments are announced or public notices are mailed to you, or can be obtained from the county for a small duplication fee.

APPRAISAL REPORT. This is a report by an appraiser rendering an opinion on the market value of your property.

IMPROVEMENTS

PLANS AND SPECIFICATIONS. The description and drawings of your improvement, whether prepared professionally or sketched by you, should be kept in your files.

BUILDING PERMIT. This is the permit document issued by the county upon approval of your plan.

INSPECTION RECORD. This is the notice indicating that an inspection has been conducted by local authorities.

ESTIMATES. Written estimates submitted by contractors for your home improvement. These can be discarded once the job has been completed to your satisfaction.

CONTRACT. This is the agreement signed by you and the contractor, spelling out all terms and conditions.

RECORD OF PAYMENTS. This refers to all checks and receipts, or a written ledger indicating the dates, the amounts paid, and the type of work performed.

INVOICES. Invoices are proof of payment for any expense you incur related to your home improvement. If you act as your own contractor, this will include materials, labor costs, and subcontractor fees.

PRELIMINARY LIEN NOTICES. These documents mailed to you by subcontractors and suppliers should be kept in your files.

LIEN RELEASES. These are the releases sent to you when you have fully paid subcontractors and suppliers, as well as the unconditional lien release signed by the general contractor.

NOTICE OF COMPLETION. A copy of the notice that is filed and recorded with your county upon completion of a home improvement.

OTHER HOUSE EXPENSES

You also should hold on to all records regarding upkeep, or general maintenance, of your home. This can include such things as painting of a room, garden maintenance, repairs to plumbing and electrical systems, and the purchase of furniture, carpeting, drapes, and appliances.

Keep records for all these items until they need redoing or replacing. While none are deductible on your income tax return or go into computing the adjusted basis of your home, at least you will have a record of any warranties or guarantees included as part of the materials or installation. This information can be important in the event of a casualty. If a fire damaged your home, you would have to establish the cost of replacement of your possessions for your insurance carrier. Invoices can help.

26

HOW HOME SALES ARE TAXED

One of the chief benefits of owning your own house, condo, or co-op is that, if you plan carefully, you probably will not have to pay taxes on the profits when you eventually sell it. This boon results from the tax law which, as in the past, allows all homeowners to defer paying taxes on the profits they make when they sell a principal residence. The new tax law retains the once-in-a-lifetime exclusion for homeowners aged 55 or older, allowing them to make a profit of up to $125,000 on the sale of a principal residence before they must start paying taxes.

A "principal" (or primary) residence is the home you live in most of the time, and includes condos and co-ops as well as single-family dwellings. If you own two houses and use each one for part of the year, the one used by you the most qualifies for the favorable tax treatment covered here.

CAPITAL GAINS

We all pay taxes on most income, whether from salaries, self-employment, tips, interest, dividends, alimony, or gains from the sale of property.

Beginning in 1988, all gains from the sale of your principal residence (which you do not postpone or exclude) will be taxed at the same rate as your other income. However, for 1987, the prior tax law applies (with certain modifications). Gain from the sale of a residence which you have owned for more than six months (a long-term capital gain) is taxable at a maximum federal rate of 28 percent. Gains from the sale of a residence owned six months or less (a short-term capital gain) is taxable at the maximum federal rate of 38.5 percent.

Under both the new tax law and the prior tax law (which remains generally applicable in 1987), a loss incurred on the sale of a home is not deductible.

ONCE-IN-A-LIFETIME EXCLUSION

The rationale for the once-in-a-lifetime exclusion rule is that older people, who often live on a fixed income, should not be hit with a large tax bill that will take away a big portion of their profit from the sale of a residence. Under current tax laws, up to $125,000 in profits from the sale of a house, condo, or co-op can be excluded from taxable income for each individual or married couple; if you are married and filing separately, you are allowed $62,500 each.

You must be 55 or older as of the date of sale, and you must have owned and lived in the house as your principal residence for at least three of the previous five years, ending on the date of sale. For a married couple who hold property jointly and file a joint return for the year of sale, either the husband or wife can satisfy the age, ownership, and use requirements in order for both to qualify for this exclusion. But if one of the spouses previously elected to exclude gain on a sale of a house after July 26, 1978, the provision cannot be used again.

Example: A house is sold for $184,000 less closing costs of $13,000, meaning that the amount realized was $171,000. The home originally cost $63,000 plus closing costs of $2,000, for an adjusted basis of $65,000. The profit was $106,000:

sales price	$184,000
closing costs	13,000
amount realized	171,000
original cost	63,000
plus original closing costs on purchase	2,000
adjusted purchase price	65,000
profit	106,000

But the seller was over 55 and elected to use her once-in-a-lifetime exclusion. Hence none of the profit was taxed, as it was lower than $125,000.

There are two exceptions to the once-in-a-lifetime rule: You cannot take advantage of this provision for any portion of your house used as a home office or for any portion rented out to someone else. The nonpersonal use of a home substantially reduces the advantages of the exclusion and in the long run can cost more in taxes than the homeowner has saved from year to year.

These exceptions do not apply if you vacate your home and rent it out temporarily while you are preparing to sell it.

DEFERRING TAXES

The other substantial tax benefit in owning and then selling your own home is the deferral feature allowed under the tax rules.

In most cases, when you buy and sell capital assets, each transaction is taxed as it is completed. As soon as an asset is sold, it is subject to tax. In the case of a principal residence, however, you are allowed to carry the gain over to your next house.

This means that even when you make a profit on the sale of a house, in most circumstances you do not have to pay taxes until later, as long as you buy another house. You can defer the gain as many times in your life as you want, except that you generally cannot roll over and defer profits more than once during a two-year period.

The following limitations apply:

1. Just as rental and home office spaces are excluded from the once-in-a-lifetime exclusion, they are excluded from the deferral provision of the tax laws.

2. You must ordinarily buy and occupy a new home within a period beginning two years before and ending two years after the sale of your old home.

3. The new home must be your new principal residence.

4. You must buy a new house, condo, or co-op whose price is greater than the adjusted sales price of the old residence. (The adjusted sales price of your old residence is equal to the sales price of the old residence less any expenses incurred in fixing up the old house for a sale.) If you buy a home that costs less than what you sold your old home for, a portion of the gain will be taxed in the year of sale. Thus, if you sell for $92,000 and the basis was $27,000 (a gain of $65,000), and you buy a new house costing $86,000, you will pay tax on $6,000:

Sales price, old house	$92,000
Purchase price, new house	86,000
Amount of gain taxed this year	6,000
Amount of gain deferred	59,000

You eventually will be liable for tax on all the profit you realize in buying and selling houses—except for what you can shelter under the one-time exclusion rule. The gain is deferred by adjusting the basis. In the previous example, the tax basis on your new house normally would be the purchase price (with adjustments), or $86,000. However, because you are deferring $59,000 in profits, the adjustment for the new house is different:

Original basis	$86,000
Profits deferred	59,000
Adjusted basis in new house	27,000

You can see how deferral works by imagining the difference this makes when your new house is sold. If that house, costing $86,000, sells for $100,000, there is a gain of $14,000. However, because the basis has been adjusted down to $27,000 (purchase price of $86,000 minus deferred gain of $59,000), the taxable profit actually is $73,000, consisting of:

Profit on sale of house	$14,000
Deferred gain	59,000
Taxable gain	73,000

Fixing-up expenses are defined as expenses that make a house more saleable but are not capital improvements. These expenses can include the cost of painting, wallpapering, decorating, sprucing up the front yard, and making general repairs. In order to be considered part of the adjusted sales price, such work must be performed during the 90-day period preceding the day the contract for the sale is signed, and all such expenses must be paid in full no later than 30 days after the closing on the house.

TRADING UP

This aspect of the tax laws has made trading up—buying progressively more expensive homes—attractive, since:

- It allows you to defer all gains.
- It enables you to build a larger investment base for larger future profits.
- It enables you and your family to improve your life-style and home environment.

It is not unrealistic for a family to own and sell several houses over their lifetimes and never pay taxes on the profit. Let's say the first house is purchased at age 28 and sold at age 33. (The average first-time buyer remains in a home 4.7 years.) The second house is kept for 10 years and sold when the homeowner is 43. At age 60, that house is sold and replaced with a condominium. That's three homes in 32 years.

The first house was bought for $28,175 (after adjustments) and is sold for $79,250. The profit of $51,075 is deferred with the purchase of another house within two years.

The basis in the second house is reduced by the profit in the first ($94,450 minus $51,075 = $43,375). This house is sold for $108,190. The profit of $64,815 (adjusted sales price minus adjusted basis) is again carried over to a third house, which again was bought within two years from sale.

This third house is purchased for $121,200. (Note that in each case the purchase price of the new house is higher than the sales price of the old, allowing deferral of all profits.) After adjustment for the deferred gain, the adjusted basis in this final house is $56,385. It is sold for $176,700, for a final profit of $120,315.

As long as the owner is over age 55 and has not previously used the once-in-a-lifetime exclusion, the entire profit is free from income tax, as it is less than $125,000.

Whenever you sell a house, you are required to file an information schedule with your income tax return. Form 2119, "Sale or Exchange of Principal Residence," includes three sections dealing with:

1. Gain and adjusted sales price
2. Gain to be postponed (deferred) and adjusted basis of new residence
3. 55 and over exclusion, gain to be reported, and adjusted basis of new residence

This form must be filed in the year a house is sold whether or not you have replaced it with another house. You have two years to qualify for the tax deferral, so if you are planning to buy or build a new house, you complete only the first section of the form. The gain is not included on your tax return.

When you do complete the replacement within the two-year period, you send an amended Form 2119. The statute of limitations for reporting a home sale will not run unless the sale and replacement is reported to the IRS.

If you originally plan not to replace your house and you report and pay tax on your gain but later buy or build within the two-year period, you can apply for a refund by filing Form 1040X.

PLANNING YOUR HOME SALE

It pays to be aware of the tax rules on a home sale starting from the time you move into your first home. It can save you a lot of money.

For example, if you plan to sell your house and rent for three or four years, think of the consequences of not being able to defer taxes on your gain. If you alter your plans to two years or less of renting before you buy another house, you can take advantage of these very favorable tax rules.

If you're near age 55 and would like to sell your house and rent or buy a smaller and less expensive house, think about waiting a year or two until you qualify for the once-in-a-lifetime exclusion. If you have substantial equity built up in your house and you bought it for a lot less than it is worth today, you can cut taxes by several thousand dollars by delaying the sale.

Be sure to consult with a professional tax accountant or tax attorney *before* you sell your house. The advice you'll receive will probably save you more in taxes than you'll pay in fees.

27

COMPUTING YOUR BASIS

"Basis" is a term used for tax purposes, and includes the buyer's total cost for the house, plus any minor adjustments used for computing capital gain or loss. It is figured in the same way it is for any other asset. If you buy a used car that isn't in perfect running order, you will have to spend money on parts and repair now and probably in the future. You will have to pay an automobile registration fee and, in many states, a sales tax. By the time you're through, your total outlay for the car is much higher than the original purchase price.

The same applies when you buy a house. Some of the closing costs must be taken into account and, if you improve the property several times, the basis rises with each capital improvement. Your basis will also change if you rent part of the house, or use part of it as a home office.

Basis is important because it determines, on the sale of the house, the gain on which you must eventually pay income tax. Naturally, from a tax perspective, the homeowner wants as small a gain as possible—that means you want to increase your reported basis as much as you legally can. Furthermore, under the new tax law, basis is important generally in determining how much interest you may deduct with respect to the debt you incur if you refinance or place a second mortgage on your home after August 16, 1986.

WHAT CAN YOU INCLUDE?

Only some of the closing costs can be used to compute the adjusted basis on your house. Points, insurance premiums, and prorated expenses such as property taxes are considered part of the general expense of owning a home and cannot be included as part of the overall cost. On the other hand, expenses such as inspections, licenses, title search fees, and recording fees are considered part of the basis.

Similarly, only capital improvements can be used to compute the basis of your house, not routine maintenance expenses. Repairing a broken fence, painting a bedroom or hallway, or cleaning a furnace are not considered capital improvements. But adding a room, installing solar heating panels, and converting a garage to a family room are considered improvements, since these projects permanently increase the value of your property.

DRAWBACKS OF OVER-IMPROVEMENT

If you plan to live in your house for many years, go ahead and make those improvements to it that will satisfy you and your family. But be aware that if you improve the house beyond its reasonable market value and try to sell it only a few years after purchase, you may not realize a profit. You may suffer a loss, and losses on principal residential properties are not deductible. Consider the following example:

Original cost		$62,000
Plus:	closing costs	1,400
Plus:	additional bathroom	11,450
	remodeled kitchen	14,600
	additional bedroom	21,895
Adjusted basis		111,345
Sales price (adjusted)		104,500
Loss on sale		6,845

In other words, an adjusted cost basis doesn't necessarily have anything to do with market value. Anyone who has observed real estate prices over the last decade knows that over a period of time properties usually rise in value. However, if a home is over-improved beyond its location and current market value, then additions to its cost basis don't add up to a profitable sale.

Of course, some improvements are better investments than others. A remodeled kitchen or bathroom will certainly increase your home's cost basis and marketability. If you have only one bathroom, adding a second one will probably return you dollar for dollar upon the sale of the house.

However, if you own a standard three-bedroom home with two baths and a garage, the reasonable market value is limited to the sale prices of other homes in the immediate area with similar features and property. If you've chosen to add a swimming pool, overhaul the heating and air-conditioning systems, and remodel the kitchen and both baths, you've put a great deal of money into the house and may not be able to demand much more on the market than for the house across the street with none of those extras. Your over-improved house may sell more easily, but it's doubtful that all of the costs of the improvements can be recovered.

Similarly, not every practical addition to the cost basis will immediately raise the market value of the house. If a new bedroom cost you $20,000, you won't always be able to sell your house for $20,000 more within a year or two. It may take three or more years before that expense can be recovered, depending on the rate of inflation and market conditions in your area. However, if your house is valued *under* the market, and you carefully choose your improvement project, the cost basis of your home can be profitably increased.

28

RENTAL PROPERTY

Buying a home is always a major investment, whether you plan to occupy the house yourself or rent it out to tenants. Every homeowner, for instance, must spend money on decorating, landscaping, and maintaining the house and grounds in good condition if he or she hopes to retain the market value of the property. The owner who rents also must keep up the property. Often a landlord is able to deduct all the maintenance expenses on an income tax return, and claim depreciation deductions additionally. These beneficial aspects of owning rental property are discussed later in this chapter.

RESPONSIBILITIES OF A LANDLORD

But first let's look at the drawbacks and responsibilities of being a landlord, especially for those who purchase property strictly for investment purposes.

In the most ideal situation, the landlord-to-be finds a reasonably priced house in a well-kept neighborhood; the house will definitely appreciate in value with very little effort on his or her part. An ideal tenant appears, who takes pride in keeping the landlord's property in top shape, working in the yard and even spending some of his own money to do so. In reality, however, you're likely to spend more money than you expected in order to keep the house and property in good condition. Your tenant will call you to complain when an appliance breaks down; he or she may badger you constantly about replacing bathroom fixtures or modernizing the kitchen appliances. The tenant may fail to maintain your house properly or may even damage it, not caring about its potential market value. Or the tenant may fail to pay the rent, while you will have to continue making your regular mortgage and tax payments on the property. Finally, the tenant may just up and leave one day, depriving you of rental income for possibly a long period of time.

A prospective landlord should also be aware that some properties require a lot more work and attention than others, depending on the size of the house, the type and extent of yard maintenance needed, and the expectations of the tenants. While you still may be able to claim some tax benefits on your real estate investment, you're also taking an equivalent risk that the house will become a headache, cost you much more than expected, and fail to grow in value.

Moreover, while a resident owner has an immediate interest in maintaining his or her house and seeing that everything is kept in good order, a landlord tends to have a very different attitude toward spending money on tenants' needs. This natural reluctance to expend funds must be balanced against the obligations of a responsible and fair landlord as well as the necessity of keeping up the value of the property pending a possible future sale.

Remember that, as a landlord, you will have to carry fire insurance and liability coverage at a substantially higher rate than is charged for a single-family house. Tenants are expected to provide their own personal property coverage, but you will be responsible for all insurance on the building itself. The income you receive from rents will probably just about cover such insurance as well as taxes, maintenance expenses, and monthly mortgage payments. You will probably save very little from the rents you receive; your expenses may well be higher than the income from the rents.

This disparity will not be critical if the tax benefits of ownership offset these cash flow considerations. However, the new tax law restricts these benefits (see information on depreciation later on in this chapter). Furthermore, even if these tax benefits remain available to you, you still can have major cash flow problems if a tenant stops paying rent, or if you have an unexpected vacancy for a long period of time.

PROTECTION FOR THE LANDLORD

As a landlord, you can protect yourself to some degree by carefully screening all tenant applications, asking for references, and checking with the tenant's previous landlord. A detailed rental lease that clearly spells out the rights and obligations of a tenant also will help—if a tenant fails to pay the rent or damages your property, you will have some grounds to initiate eviction proceedings.

A landlord also can avoid many headaches by hiring a professional management service to screen tenants, get leases signed, collect rents, and monitor the condition and upkeep of the property. A management service protects the owner's privacy and acts as a buffer between landlord and tenant. If a tenant has a request or complaint, he or she goes to the management service, not directly to the landlord. If a vacancy occurs, you won't have to advertise, show the unit, or go through the process of approving the renters. The service will take care of all that for you.

Usually a management service will charge you either a flat fee or a percentage of the rents you receive—sometimes a minimum monthly fee is part of the agreement. If you have more than two rental units, a management service is well worth the price. The cost usually can be deducted as a business expense when you compute your taxes. However you should be aware that if you transfer *all* management and operational responsibilities to a management service, you will not be treated by the IRS as "actively participating" in the rental real estate activity for tax purposes. Thus you will not be able to take advantage of the new tax law allowing you to deduct up to $25,000 in rental real estate losses against your income from other sources (see pages 189 and 190). If you otherwise qualify for this relief provision, you may wish to structure your relationship with the management service so that you are "actively participating" in the rental of your property.

Participation includes making management decisions such as approving tenants, lease terms, capital expenditures, and arranging for others to provide services for your property. For example, you would stipulate to your management company that you must approve any repair costs over $100, except in emergency situations. It's also helpful if you, not your management service, personally pay all mortgage and tax bills on the property.

REPORTING TO THE IRS

Money received from rental property is reported on your income tax return as a source of income, and the net profit or loss—total rents received minus allowed expenses—is reported along with any other sources of income.

Currently, any profit or loss is reported on IRS Schedule E "Supplemental Income Schedule." First, describe your property and then report your total rental income in the appropriate column. Following that, list your expenses. These expenses probably include:

- advertising: payments for rental listings in the newspapers
- auto and travel: the cost of traveling to your investment property to inspect it, meet with tenants, or collect rents
- cleaning and maintenance: the upkeep of the property, including lawn and yard maintenance, window washing, carpet cleaning, painting, as well as physical repairs and replacements
- commissions: money paid to a real estate agency for locating a tenant for your rental property
- insurance: the premiums you pay for casualty and liability coverage on the property
- interest: the amount paid on your rental property's mortgage during a given tax year
- management service: cost of hiring a management service to help you manage your property
- legal and other professional fees: the cost of preparing and approving rental and lease contracts, retaining the services of an accountant or tax advisor, etc.
- repairs: funds expended for repair of the house and its attachments or fixtures
- supplies: the cost of stationery for rental purposes, bookkeeping materials, etc.
- taxes: property tax payments
- utilities: cost of gas and electric, water, or waste disposal services
- wages and salaries: your payments to gardeners, maintenance people, and others on your payroll who manage or operate your rental property
- other: any other expense that is normal, reasonable, and necessary in the operation of your rental property
- depreciation: the allowable annual write-off based on the building's cost (land cannot be depreciated). Depreciation is summarized on the next page and explained in detail in the instructions for form 4562 of the federal income tax return.

The difference between rents received and your total expenses is your profit—or loss. A profit is added to your other income. Deduction of losses is limited under the new tax law, except that you may be able to deduct up to $25,000 in rental losses depending on the extent of your participation in the management of your property, and your income level. See "Effects of the New Tax Law on Real Estate Investment" below.

DEPRECIATION

Depreciation is the gradual decrease, on paper, in the market value of property due to age, wear and tear, or market conditions. It is a noncash expense. You don't actually spend money to claim this deduction, but a portion of the value of the house or condo is taken as a depreciation deduction each year. In fact, even though the house or condo probably is growing in value, you still can claim such a depreciation deduction on your income tax. Depreciation thus allows you to show a lowered profit or, in many cases, a loss for tax purposes even when you take in more cash than you pay out. This type of deduction is quite legal and is the investment attraction of improved real estate in any form—houses, apartments, or industrial and commercial property. However, the overall benefit of this depreciation deduction has been reduced or modified by the new tax law, which may preclude a deduction of any real estate losses, depending on your income level and the extent of your participation in the management of the property.

Under the new tax law, residential rental real estate placed in service after December 31, 1986, is depreciated over a 27.5-year recovery period; commercial real estate is depreciated over a 31.5-year recovery period. This means that you can write off the full value of the house or condo (excluding the value of the land) over 27.5 years, and no less. By calculating your annual depreciation deduction by using the straight-line method, you deduct the same amount each year for depreciation, except during the first year when only a prorated deduction is allowed.

EFFECTS OF THE NEW TAX LAW ON REAL ESTATE INVESTMENT

While the tax advantages from investing in rental real estate have been greatly reduced under the new law, some benefits still remain for those small investors who directly purchase and manage their investment properties. The new tax law classifies losses from rental real estate as "passive" losses. You can no longer use such passive losses to offset other income such as your salary, dividends, and interest you receive. But you can use such losses to offset other passive income—i.e., income from other real estate investments or from limited partnership interests. You may carry forward passive losses that cannot be deducted in a particular year, and deduct them in a later year in which you have passive income. Or you may choose to dispose of your investment entirely.

> Example: In 1987 you received $85,000 in salary income and $5,000 in interest and dividends. In addition, you report a $10,000 loss from a limited real estate partnership interest you bought in 1987. (The limited partnership owns a new shopping mall.) Under the passive loss rules, you may not use the $10,000 loss from your limited partnership interest to reduce your salary and investment income. Thus if you own no other real estate investments or limited partnership interests, you may not claim the partnership loss in 1987, but must carry it forward, for an indefinite period.
>
> Generally speaking, if in a succeeding year you report passive income from the limited partnership interest or from any other real estate investment, you may apply the $10,000 loss to offset such income. Otherwise, you may only claim the loss if you dispose of your limited partnership interest at a loss.

Congress provided limited relief for taxpayers who were holding real estate and other passive investments on October 22, 1986. If you were holding a rental property investment on that date, you may deduct 65 percent of your net losses from such an investment in 1987, 40 percent in 1988, 20 percent in 1989, and 10 percent in 1990.

Congress provided further relief for small investors—mainly landlords and owners of small rental properties. If you own rental real estate and "actively participate" in its operation and management, you may deduct up to $25,000 of net losses, but your adjusted gross income must be $100,000 or less (computed without including any taxable social security benefits and before deducting any passive losses or contributions to an IRA account). If your adjusted gross income is between $100,000 and $150,000, your deductible loss is decreased by an amount equal to one-half the amount of income above $100,000. So if your adjusted gross is $116,000 before taking the loss, you could deduct up to $17,000 in rental losses, or $25,000 minus $8,000. Those with an income above $150,000 cannot deduct such losses at all.

In order to be considered as actively participating in a rental real estate activity you must own at least a 10 percent interest in the investment. Furthermore, if you are only a limited partner, the IRS will not treat you as an active participant. In addition, you must actually take part in making management decisions or arranging for others to provide services (such as repairs) in the real estate venture. While the Treasury has not yet issued regulations on this point, participation probably includes approving new tenants, deciding on rental terms, and approving capital or repair expenditures. Using an agent to carry out your decisions will not necessarily disqualify you.

The new tax law also adds a second limit on the deduction of losses from rental real estate. Under the new law you may only deduct losses up to the amount for which you are "at-risk." This at-risk amount includes the amount you would lose if the venture failed, and thus includes your own cash investment and any debts for which you are personally liable. In addition, the at-risk amount generally includes mortgages loaned by banks and other financial institutions even if you are not personally liable for the mortgage debt. The principal effect of the at-risk rule is to limit losses on properties bought largely with "seller financing," that is, when the seller finances a portion of the selling price.

As you can see, tax reform has greatly increased the complexity of the tax law applicable to real estate investment. Most importantly, any tax benefits you enjoy from a real estate investment depend heavily on your own personal tax picture. Therefore, it is advisable that you consult with an accountant or tax advisor *before* making any type of real estate investment.

NEGATIVE OR POSITIVE CASH FLOW?

The following scenario illustrates the extent to which the new tax law impacts on real estate investment: In 1988 you purchase and actively manage a building that produces the following financial results for the year:

Total rental income	$8,000
Cash expenses (includes mortgage interest)	9,000
Depreciation	3,000
Payments to principal (first year)	200
Cash flow	[$1,200]

In this case, your adjusted gross income for the year, not including this particular real estate activity, is $85,000. You do not own any other properties, or partnership interests. The above figures show that you have a negative cash flow from your rental property of $1,200 (the combination of cash expenses and payments to principal less income).

Taking depreciation into account, you have a potential loss of $4,000:

Income	$8,000
Minus cash expenses	−9,000
Minus depreciation	−3,000
Loss	[$4,000]

However, since the $4,000 can be deducted on your income tax return, you save $1,320 in the 33 percent tax bracket (33 percent of $4,000). When that is taken into account, your true cash flow is positive:

Negative cash flow	− $1,200
Tax benefit	+ 1,320
Net positive cash flow	+ $ 120

If your adjusted gross income for 1988 were $146,000 (before including your loss from this transaction) you can deduct only $2,000 of the loss: $25,000 − (.5 × [146,000 − 100,000]) = $2,000. In this case, your cash flow would remain negative:

Negative cash flow	− $1,200
Tax benefit ($2,000 × .33)	+ 660
Negative cash flow	[$540]

As you can see, under the new tax law, it becomes more important than in the past for you to consider the economics (i.e., cash return) of a rental property before deciding to invest.

THE PATIENT INVESTOR

Today there are numerous get-rich-quick schemes, publicized in books and on television, that seek to persuade the eager novice that investment in real estate can make almost anyone a millionaire in a comparatively short time. Often these blueprints for riches suggest that you can profitably invest in property by leveraging your equity—borrowing money to buy one property and then using the equity in that house in order to buy another, and so on—continuing the buying and selling indefinitely and hopefully amassing more and more money in the process. Or some real estate pitchmen may push the idea that fortunes easily can be made by buying foreclosed homes or handyman specials, fixing them up, and then selling them at a huge profit.

There's a problem with all these grandiose plans. You can't get rich quickly in real estate unless you're extremely lucky both in the property you choose for investment and in market conditions prevailing at the time you buy. Foreclosed and poorly maintained houses usually have many problems that can be remedied only by large infusions of time and money. In other words, more of your money has to be invested just to stay ahead of the immediate cash demands.

Unless you are an experienced professional wheeler-dealer or a reckless go-for-broke gambler, don't even think of leveraging your equity. Finance your real estate investments separately. Don't risk losing your own home for the supposed profits of real estate speculation.

Certainly it is possible to mortgage one property to the hilt in order to finance the purchase of another piece of real estate. This investment technique may work out quite well if it is done intelligently, as part of a carefully worked out, professional design. But there are too many pitfalls in the leveraged-equity scheme with which the inexperienced nonprofessional must deal, including problem houses that remain a problem, unexpected expenses, difficult and unreliable tenants—all increasing the risks that a severe cash flow crisis could develop, leading to major losses and possible bankruptcy.

Don't be tempted by unfounded promises of easy wealth in real estate. Landlording can be a financially rewarding form of investment, but it is also one that requires constant attention and hard work. Its many frustrations, inconveniences, and cash flow risks are often the price you pay for an eventual worthwhile venture. But until you have serious, long-term experience as a landlord, it's highly advisable to keep your investments at a reasonable level.

VACATION HOMES

At some time, many homeowners consider buying a second home—for the enjoyment of owning a getaway place in the mountains, on a lake, or near the beach, to save money on expensive vacations elsewhere, or as a profitable investment for the future. But the potential vacation home investor should keep in mind that the market today is both complex and changing, and often such a purchase brings unexpected headaches and financial burdens that may eventually outweigh any potential benefits.

Before buying, ask yourself these questions: Do you really want to commit to spending most of your vacations in one place? Do you want the year-round upkeep and responsibilities of a property you may only use seasonally? How long or difficult is the trip to your property—especially during peak vacation season traffic? Do you have the temperament to cope with the demands of furnishing and maintaining two households—possibly including the needs of family and pets? And what about the relatives and friends who may be eager to enjoy your vacation home along with you?

Of course, many people feel refreshed by a change of scene from one home environment to another and do not mind the burdens of a second household. Frequently, such buyers purchase their second homes as future retirement residences or for a much-needed break from urban wear and tear. But every vacation home buyer should cultivate a hard-headed attitude toward his or her potential Shangri-la; without careful planning and a realistic outlook, the purchase of a second home can become an emotional and financial drain.

RENTING OUT YOUR VACATION HOME

Often people buy a second home with the thought of renting it out for a good price in the most desirable vacation month, or in the off-season when they won't be using it themselves. They hope to get a good tax break in the bargain. But the Tax Reform Act of 1986 has complicated that expectation for many second-home buyers.

For federal tax purposes you must treat a vacation home as a personal residence if you use it for personal use for a number of days which exceeds the greater of (a) 14 days or (b) 10% of the number of days during the year for which the home is rented at a fair rental price. If you use a vacation home as a residence and rent it out for less than 15 days during the year, you may not deduct any rental expenses and need not report any rental income. *However, you may still deduct taxes and mortgage interest to the same extent as if you received no rental income.* Thus, if you itemize your deductions, you may ordinarily deduct on Schedule A of your Form 1040 the property taxes you pay on your second home. In addition, if the vacation home is your principal or secondary residence, you may generally deduct all mortgage interest. (See pages 92 and 93.)

If you use the vacation home as a personal residence and also rent it out for 15 days or more during the year, you must report on Schedule E any rental income you receive. However, you may not deduct all of your rental expenses. Instead, you must allocate your vacation home expenses between your personal use and the expenses of rental use. The IRS has taken the position that you must determine the portion of each of your expenses attributable to your rental use of the vacation home (other than expenses directly connected to working with tenants, such as real estate brokerage fees) by multiplying the amount of the expense by a fraction of which the numerator is the number of days the home is rented, and the denominator is the total number of days the home is used for both rental and personal purposes. The portion of each of your expenses attributable to personal use is determined in a similar manner. However, the Tax Court has ruled that you also may determine the portion of your tax and interest expense attributable to rental use by multiplying the amount of such expenses by a fraction of which the numerator is the number of days the home is rented and the denominator is 365 (days in the year). Use this allocation method if it increases the amount of your expenses deductible under the vacation home rules.

You may include as an itemized deduction on Schedule A of your income tax return the portion of the property taxes attributable to your personal use of the home, as well as the portion of your mortgage interest allocated to your personal use. Similarly, deduct on Schedule E all those taxes allocated to rental use, and on Schedule A all mortgage interest allocated to rental use. These interest deductions are subject to the same limitations that apply to any other secondary residences. (See pages 92 and 93 and the section on "How the New Tax Law Affects the Homebuyer.")

While still not entirely clear under the new tax law, it appears that you may only deduct other operating expenses (i.e., expenses other than depreciation, taxes, and interest previously deducted) to the extent that your rental income exceeds the deduction for taxes and interest allocated to the rental use of the property. If rental income exceeds the taxes, interest, and operating expenses allocated to rental use, you may deduct depreciation to the extent of such excess. However, in no event may you deduct rental expenses (other than taxes and interest) in excess of your rental income from the home. Thus, in general, if you use a vacation home as a personal residence as well, you may be unable to deduct your entire rental tax loss.

If you do not use the vacation home as a personal residence and rent out the house in a manner indicating you expect to make a profit, you may potentially deduct all your rental expenses. (Expenses, other than interest and taxes, attributable to personal use are not deductible.) However, if your rental expenses exceed rental income, the deduction of any loss is limited by the new tax rules that apply to investment property (i.e., the passive activity loss rules and at-risk rules are described on page 189 and 190).

The new tax law has prompted vacation-home owners to reconsider their tax planning. Under prior law, many taxpayers limited use of their vacation home to 14 days a year in order to deduct any rental loss from the property. Under the new law, unless taxpayers have passive income from other sources equal to such loss, they may only deduct such loss to the extent that (a) they qualify for the transition relief Congress provided for holders of investments on October 22, 1986, or (b) they have an adjusted gross income of less than $150,000 and actively participate in the operation and management of the property. (See page 190.) On the other hand, if you use a vacation home for enough days so that it qualifies as a second residence, you may at least be able to deduct all taxes and mortgage interest paid (even if these expenses exceed rental income).

Example 1 On January 1, 1988, you purchase a vacation condominium for $150,000, paying $30,000 in cash and obtaining a mortgage for $120,000. You use the condominium for 10 days during the year and rent it out for 90 days to an unrelated party. Your income and expenses for the year are as follows:

	Total	(90%) Business	(10%) Personal
Total rental income	5,000	5,000	-0-
Taxes*	(2,000)	(1,800)	(200)
Mortgage interest*	(12,000)	(10,800)	(1,200)
Common charges	(2,000)	(1,800)	(200)
Depreciation	(5,000)	(4,500)	(500)
	(16,000)	(13,900)	(2,100)

Your adjusted gross income for the year, not including this activity, is $165,000. You have no other passive income or losses.

In this case you have potential loss of $13,900 from rental of the condominium. However, your deduction of this loss is barred by the new passive activity loss rules.

You may deduct on Schedule A $680 attributable to your personal use of the property ($200 of the taxes and $480 of mortgage interest, representing 40 percent of the $1,200 of mortgage interest allocated to personal use).

Example 2 Same facts as Example 1, except that you use the condominium for 20 days in 1988 and rent it to unrelated parties for only 80 days (at the same total rent).

You designate the condominium as your secondary residence for purposes of deducting mortgage interest. Your income and expense for tax purposes are as follows:

	Total	(80%) Business	(20%) Personal
Total rental income	5,000	5,000	-0-
Taxes*	(2,000)	(1,600)	(400)
Mortgage interest*	(12,000)	(9,600)	(2,400)
Net	(9,000)	(6,200)	(2,800)
Common charges	(2,000)	(1,600)	(400)
Depreciation	(5,000)	(4,000)	(1,000)
	(16,000)	(11,800)	(4,200)

In this case, you may deduct at least $14,000 of expenses on your return yielding deductions in excess of income of $9,000. You may deduct on Schedule E $1,600 of taxes as a rental expense. You may also deduct on Schedule A the remainder of your tax expense ($400) and the entire mortgage interest expense ($12,000).

Example 3 Same facts as Example 1, except that you have adjusted gross income of only $75,000 before considering your loss from this activity. You have no other income or losses from real estate ventures or other passive activities. You actively participate in the management of the condominium.

In this case you may deduct on Schedule E your entire loss of $13,800 from rental of the condominium in addition to your deduction of $680 of taxes and interest on Schedule A.

In sum, under the new tax law you may wish to reconsider whether you should limit use of your vacation home to less than fifteen days a year.

*IRS allocation method used.

OTHER WAYS TO OWN A HOME

29

MOBILE HOMES

Today there are an estimated 8.5 million people living in 4 million mobile home units throughout the United States. This figure does not include those who live in vans, campers, and trailers, which are considered motor vehicles in most states.

Mobile homes are popular with first-time home buyers, many of whom cannot afford to buy any other kind of property. This form of housing is also attractive to older couples whose children have grown and left home. Many of these "empty-nesters" no longer need a full-size house or want to pay for the increasing costs of house maintenance and utilities. Moreover, many elderly people find that the kind of community living available in mobile home parks has definite social advantages.

TAX CONSIDERATIONS

The 1980 Federal Housing Act states that mobile homes should be called "manufactured homes." However, because "mobile home" is the more popular term, it will be used throughout this chapter. Technically, a mobile home is not real estate, but is rather a form of personal property, like an automobile, boat, or a piece of furniture. Even so, you can sell a house and move to a mobile home and still qualify for the deferral-of-gain tax rule as long as the mobile home contains cooking, sleeping, and sanitation facilities and can be categorized as your primary residence. You are also allowed to deduct loan interest and property taxes for mobile homes on your federal income tax return according to the rules of the 1986 Tax Reform Act pertaining to primary residences.

At present the new tax law is unclear regarding the possibility of deducting loan interest and property taxes on your mobile home if it is a secondary residence or vacation home. For more information on this matter, consult your tax accountant or lawyer.

INSURANCE CONSIDERATIONS

Most mobile-home owners buy a form of insurance similar to the HO-2 form that protects homeowners against 18 potential casualties. Many of these mobile home policies include extra coverage for earthquake and flood damage that normally wouldn't be available to most homeowners.

In some areas, however, wind damage is specifically excluded from these insurance policies. In the Atlantic and Gulf states of North Carolina, South Carolina, Florida, Alabama, Mississippi, Louisiana, and Texas—all those states where hurricane damage can be fairly frequent and severe—a special additional form of beach and windstorm insurance must be purchased above and beyond the standard policy.

Some states have so-called tie-down regulations requiring that mobile homes be securely anchored to the ground; insurance carriers also require tie-downs in the most storm-prone regions. In some parts of the country, insurers will offer special discounts for tie-downs, even if such safety precautions are not ordinarily required. Also excluded from many insurance policies for mobile homes are such add-ons as awnings, porches, and air-conditioning equipment.

Ironically, only about 2 percent of all mobile homes are moved once they're secured in the owner's lot—many are anchored to a permanent foundation. However, if you do move a mobile home, your insurance will not be in effect during the move or in the new location. Before relocating, make sure to arrange for two types of coverage: special collision insurance for the move, and one that will protect you in the new site.

The usual terms of the standard mobile-home policy are similar to the provisions of a homeowner's policy. Unless you request higher limits, you can expect coverage of 50 percent of the value of the mobile home plus your possessions, an allowance of $15 per day for additional living expenses in case of loss, and $25,000 of liability protection. Most insurers will provide mobile home insurance coverage for units that are 10 feet by 40 feet or larger, and cost $4,000 or more when new.

FINANCING AND MARKET VALUES

As personal property, mobile homes are financed more like automobiles than like houses. Your loan most likely will be at a higher rate and for a shorter term than the usual home mortgage.

Lenders consider a 30-year mortgage for a mobile home totally out of the question. Ten years generally is the maximum term allowed, and interest runs at least 2 percentage points higher than the going rate for a home mortgage. The reason is simple: Mobile homes tend to decrease in value rather than increase as houses traditionally do. Consequently, lenders' risks are higher, and they want their loans to be repaid as soon as possible. In fact, many lenders who gladly finance or refinance single-family houses will have nothing to do with mobile homes as a matter of policy.

While you'll pay less in total interest over a shorter mortgage term than you would over a long one for a house, the higher rate and higher monthly payment can be a strain on your budget, especially when they are added to the lot fees you have to pay to the mobile home park. Some lenders stretch out their terms for the larger, better-built mobile homes that are becoming increasingly popular. Unlike the traditional metal units, these mobile homes are likely to have wood walls, roofs, and floors and the construction quality generally is higher, along with the price tag.

The Federal Housing Administration and the Veterans Administration offer low-interest 15-year mobile-home loans. Again, the higher the quality of construction the better the financing terms.

The investment value of a mobile home depends largely on the quality of the unit and where it is situated. Typically, a traditional standard-sized mobile home loses 20 to 50 percent of its value in the first five years. However, the new wooden mobile homes look more like single-family houses, wear better, and hold value longer than the older models. Manufacturers more often set mobile homes on subdivision lots and sell the land with the unit. This is bound to boost the investment value.

Obviously, an unpaved mobile-home park that is full of old depreciated units, crowded between other lots, and backed by a busy freeway or railroad track is a highly undesirable place to live. A peaceful, patrolled, well-kept park with paved streets, adequate space between units, with a swimming pool, and a recreation center will cost the individual homeowner more but also will enhance the values of all the mobile homes in that particular area.

ADVANTAGES AND DISADVANTAGES

Mobile homes offer several advantages:

1. They cost less. A typical mobile home measuring 14 feet by 69 feet can be purchased for $20,000 and up. A double-wide unit measuring 24 feet by 64 feet or larger can be purchased for as little as $28,000. These units typically contain two bedrooms, a family room, a living room, a dining area, and two baths.

2. They are good starter homes. If you cannot afford to buy a single-family house, you may be able to afford a mobile home.

3. They are good investments for empty nesters. Mobile homes are cheaper and easier to maintain. Since many empty nesters are over 55, and can take advantage of the tax exclusion rules, they can sell a more expensive home and not have to pay taxes on their profit.

4. The environment of a mobile home park is well suited for frequent social contact and allows people to make new friends readily.

5. Monthly lot fees usually include water and garbage services, maintenance of common areas, and in some parks access to a clubhouse and swimming pool.

6. Quality mobile home construction is becoming more common, and a 1976 federal law requires that buyers of new units receive at least a one-year warranty on their purchase.

There are also disadvantages:

1. Mobile homes generally have a poor investment value. Lower-priced units and those parked in lower-quality lots will decline in value by as much as half the purchase price within a few years.

2. Sellers of mobile homes may have problems finding suitable buyers, since many people still shy away from this type of lifestyle. If the park is not of the highest quality, the seller is at a further disadvantage.

3. Lot fees can be periodically increased. These fees range from $50 to $600 per month, and possibly more in the highest-quality mobile home parks. Obviously, the better the environment, the higher the cost. Even if you own the land beneath your mobile home, the common maintenance fees can be periodically increased.

4. There have been some construction problems with mobile homes in the past. While manufacturers must give a one-year warranty and many offer five years, some manufacturers are slow in responding to complaints. The most common problems in mobile homes are poor insulation and leaky roofs.

5. Mobile homes are very vulnerable to fire and windstorm.

6. Financing alternatives are limited.

BUYING RECOMMENDATIONS

Here are the most important rules to follow if you are in the market for a mobile home:

CHECK THE APPEARANCE OF THE PARK. The quality of life in a mobile home park will be extremely important in the long run, so you should be willing to pay higher fees for better surroundings. Make sure streets are well paved, ample space is provided between each mobile home, and all common areas are well tended and maintained.

EXAMINE THE LOCATION. Is the park in a quiet area, well away from freeways, railroad tracks, and busy streets? You also should look for a park located close to transportation, shopping, churches, and other conveniences.

COMPARE PARK RULES AND FEES. Find out how often the fees have been increased. Be sure that park rules won't restrict your selling the mobile home later and that you won't be required to buy a specified model from only one dealer. Are there any entrance fees? If so, how much? Are there extra fees for hooking up to the utilities? For how long is the lease? What are the other park rules regarding visitors and pets?

LOOK INTO LOCAL FINANCING. Before committing yourself to buying a mobile home, visit several lenders and determine what mortgage terms are available. Shop around and don't overlook FHA and VA loans.

RESERVE A LOT SPACE BEFORE YOU BUY. Never purchase a mobile home until you have reserved a lot space in a mobile home park that you have checked out thoroughly.

BUY QUALITY CONSTRUCTION. Wood construction is preferred in a mobile home. Better-quality construction will furnish you a more comfortable home that will maintain its value longer.

EXAMINE YOUR WARRANTY. Manufacturers are required to give you a one-year warranty on a mobile home, but many offer as much as five years. Be sure you understand in advance the limitations and exclusions in the warranty of sale, and find out what the procedure for filing a warranty claim involves.

ASK ABOUT EXTRA COSTS. Will the manufacturer charge you for transporting a mobile home to your site or for setting it up? What other costs are involved? Also, if you need a mortgage, there will be closing costs; be sure to find out what they will amount to. In several states, you will have to pay sales tax and registration, which can add up.

BUY A USED MODEL. Because mobile homes are considered personal property and not real estate and because their value declines rapidly, you can usually find a well-maintained second-hand mobile home, and get more for your money. Such a used mobile home should date from after 1976, when the Department of Housing and Urban Development began requiring minimum safety and quality standards. If you buy a used model, get a written certification from the owner that the mobile home meets current HUD standards.

INSTALL SAFETY EXTRAS. Securely anchor your house whether this is required by state law or not. Install smoke detectors and fire extinguishers, especially in the kitchen area.

BUY THE RIGHT INSURANCE. Shop around for good rates, but don't hesitate to pay for extra insurance if the standard mobile home policy doesn't adequately cover your possessions or if you want higher liability protection.

30

CONDOMINIUMS AND COOPERATIVES

CONDOMINIUMS

It may be difficult to believe, but in the early 1960s "condominium" was hardly a household word—there were a few condo developments, but they were mostly in retirement or resort communities. A survey by the Department of Housing and Urban Development reveals that by 1975, 14,000 condominium developments had been built in this country, although half were located in only three states: New York, California, and Florida. By 1985, according to this same study, there were over 60,000 condominium projects in the United States, totaling more than 3 million units.

The demand for this type of housing is still growing. The National Association of Realtors reports that today one of every four new housing sales is a condominium unit and that 65 percent of all condominium buyers are first-time home purchasers.

The prices of condominiums today are on a par with the prices of single-family houses in many parts of the country. In large cities, condos are considered luxury housing, while well-constructed condo units, often in large-scale developments with pools and tennis courts, are popular housing choices in the suburbs of our large cities. Generally condos appeal to working couples buying their first home, single and divorced people, and those empty-nesters who no longer want the burdens of single-family house maintenance and upkeep. Because these units are readily available for subletting, many homeowners find condos attractive as second or vacation homes, while others consider them good investments as prime rental property.

THE CONDOMINIUM CONCEPT. The Department of Housing and Urban Development refers to condos as "air space estates." When you own a condo, you do not own the building or the land, only the air space within the walls. You own all finished surfaces on the walls (such as wallpaper) but not the walls themselves; you own light fixtures and carpeting but not the ceilings and floors. Everything *within* the confines of the unit is yours—you receive a deed for it and the exact amount of space you purchase will be recorded in the local government records office.

The rest of the development—hallways, grounds, club room, swimming pool, lobby—is called "undivided interests" and all unit owners in the condominium development use these elements communally.

THE CONDO BOARD. A condominium development is a self-governing community. While each unit is individually owned, the common interests of the development are managed and controlled collectively by the group.

A condominium association is created to elect a board of managers, sometimes called the board of directors. Each unit holder is a member of the condominium association and can vote for the board of managers. The number of votes you have depends upon the percentage of interest you hold in the property, which in turn is based upon other factors.

Some developments base the number of votes primarily on the square footage contained within the units. Voting shares can also be allocated based upon the relative desirability of a unit's location—floor level, view, or lack of proximity to traffic noise and pollution.

The board of managers' duties include:

- Establishment of an operating budget
- Collection of maintenance fees for common areas
- Enforcement of fee collections, including the right to place liens on the properties of delinquent owners
- Distribution of billings, unpaid assessment notices, and other information
- Creation and enforcement of rules concerning the use of common areas
- Conducting annual or semiannual meetings
- Acting on improvement requests from owners
- Payment of hazard and liability insurance premiums for the common areas
- Compliance with state laws

Usually the board of managers has to approve any proposed improvements to be made on a unit. In fact, it's likely that the by-laws of the association will explicitly forbid any major alterations within a unit without prior approval by the board. If the by-laws are specific in this regard, and if the board itself is not flexible, permission to make these alterations may not be easily obtained. If you plan to make major renovations in a particular unit, check the by-laws carefully *before* you buy. However, the board cannot restrict you from selling your unit to anyone you choose and cannot dictate the terms of the lease if you decide to rent out your unit. It's always best to check the by-laws—some properties retain a "right of first refusal" in which the board gets first crack at renting or buying an available unit.

The board also can enforce rules of conduct in the building including restrictions on the use of the unit for business purposes, noise after certain hours, and usage of common areas in the complex.

COOPERATIVE HOUSING

Co-ops are not a particularly popular housing alternative in the United States, except in a few large urban centers in the northeast. In the northeast, there were 135,000 co-op purchases in 1985. Of these, 82,000 were in New York State, and about three-fourths of these purchases were in the New York metropolitan area. For most Americans, condominiums are a much more popular home-owning alternative. While there are many physical similarities between condos and co-ops, there are significant technical differences as well. When you own a cooperative apartment you don't own any real property, only shares in the corporation that owns the complex. The buyer acquires shares allocated to a particular apartment, as well as a proprietary lease for the unit. Unlike condos, co-op corporations typically have an underlying mortgage on the entire property. For this reason, monthly maintenance charges for co-ops are usually higher than for condos, since the co-op owner is paying off his share of the corporation's interest on the mortgage each month. This additional cost is taken into account and, as a result, co-ops are priced somewhat lower than a comparable condo.

Voting rights in co-ops are determined in the same way as for condos. However, your financing of the shares, your rights as an investor, and some of your risks can be different. For example, financing can involve your taking on a mortgage loan, just as for a house or a condo. Many building corporations, however, have a limitation on the amount of personal financing allowed, which means you may have to come up with a good deal of cash.

Compared with condos, a co-op board has a greater degree of control over the purchasers of shares in the building corporation. A co-op board can actually approve or disapprove a prospective buyer, and can disallow subletting as well. However, some boards may be more flexible than others in this regard, especially when the owner of a unit is forced to move to another area or, for whatever reason, cannot locate a buyer for his or her shares. The co-op board also may approve a sublet on a one-time basis if it is for a specified length of time (one- or two-year lease) and the owner is necessarily absent—for instance, working abroad. As with condos, the rules and policies of the co-op corporation should be thoroughly explored before you make any commitment to buy.

Besides paying off a part of your mortgage loan each month, you will have to pay a substantial monthly maintenance fee to the building management. However, that fee covers not only the cost of maintaining the common areas and property taxes, but your share of the interest costs for the building's mortgage as well. Such costs are tax-deductible if the co-op is your primary or secondary residence.

There is always a risk that the rising cost of maintenance and labor will result in increases in the monthly maintenance rate—but this is not necessarily a problem unique to co-ops. Condo and single-family homeowners also face rising labor and upkeep costs, although owners of single-family dwellings often have the option of deferring some major repairs until finances permit their undertaking.

It's highly unlikely that you as a shareholder would ever be forced to sell your unit at a large loss because of the higher expense of maintaining it. However, it *could* happen if you make a poor choice of a co-op corporation. Before buying, have your attorney carefully review the proprietary lease, the by-laws, and all the recent financial statements of the co-op corporation, and have the building and your particular unit inspected by a professional inspector.

As a co-op investor, you have exclusive use of your apartment, as well as use of the common areas, just as you do in a condo. However, co-op boards impose restrictions on alterations or improvements to individual units. You must get permission from them for major renovations, but this approval should not be unreasonably withheld.

The interested buyer should know that there are many benefits of co-op living: tax advantages from writing off your share of the corporation's mortgage interest and real estate taxes, the economy of shared maintenance costs, the chances of a greater degree of compatibility with your immediate neighbors and, as with condos, the enjoyment of an urban life-style with a minimum of home upkeep.

BUYING A CONDO OR CO-OP

There are three ways to purchase a condominium or a cooperative apartment: You can buy a unit from an owner in an existing development or building, you can be a first buyer in a new development, or you can purchase a conversion unit as an "insider" tenant. Each of these forms of condo or co-op purchase carries its own advantages and disadvantages.

UNIT IN EXISTING DEVELOPMENT. Established condominium or co-op developments have the distinct advantage of having an operating, experienced board of managers or directors. The fact that any initial construction problems of the building or development will have been discovered and usually resolved by the time you buy your unit is another advantage to you. However, it's always wise to hire an independent home building inspector or engineer to inspect the unit before you purchase it. The inspector can also examine the building and check out its general condition and mechanical systems—there may be essential repair work pending that can cause costly assessments or a rise in maintenance fees for all the unit owners. Review the inspector's report carefully before you sign a contract to purchase. If possible, speak with the superintendent or manager to find out the building's maintenance history and if the board of managers or directors has recently voted for any maintenance increases for pending repairs. Your attorney also should carefully review the latest financial statements of the building corporation or complex. For your own protection, review the by-laws of the development with your attorney in order to ensure that you are willing to abide by all the rules and regulations of the co-op or condo management.

FIRST BUYER IN A NEW DEVELOPMENT. Buying a unit in a new development gives you the advantage of realizing any rise in market value once the development is fully occupied, assuming the demand for the units continues. (If the demand slackens, the value of the units will either remain stable or drop.) It also means that you and the other new owners will have to contend with the initial growing pains of a new real estate venture, with all its accompanying anxieties and frustrations.

In most cases, the developer or sponsor will control the existing board of managers or directors until there are enough owners to constitute a majority. Make sure that your prospectus, condominium by-laws, or proprietary lease calls for the developer to give up majority control of the board once 51 percent of the units have been sold. Otherwise, a developer can exercise control over the entire complex for an unreasonably long time. Also, before you buy, try to find out if the monthly maintenance fee is realistic. In some cases, a developer will set low maintenance fees to attract buyers (a practice called low-balling); later, when the developer has gone, the unit owners discover that they have to raise the fees considerably to cover the normal operating expenses of the complex. Check the monthly fees of any nearby established condo or co-op developments of similar size in order to compare costs and maintenance charges.

PURCHASING A CONVERSION UNIT. Many condo and co-op units were once rental apartments. If your rental building or complex is converting to condo or co-op status, you usually can purchase your unit at a lower-than-market price as an inside buyer. The conversion process is a complicated and frustrating experience for many tenants, and there are many factors to consider if you are planning to buy your apartment. The main considerations are:

1. Condition of the building(s): Are you buying someone else's headache? Will repairs and future maintenance costs drastically increase your financial burden?

2. Price of the unit: How does it compare with comparable units on the market?

3. Location of the building/complex: Does the location guarantee a continued demand for units like yours, at least for the forseeable future?

4. Current market conditions: Is there a steady demand for condo/co-op housing in your area? Is it a popular alternative to renting or buying a single-family house?

5. Your income level: Can you afford it? Will your immediate and future income level allow you to comfortably support the burden of monthly mortgage and interest costs plus maintenance fees that may escalate periodically?

If you, as a tenant, have received a "red herring" (a term meaning a proposed prospectus for a conversion plan that has been submitted to the state attorney general's office for approval), start checking out your options. First, contact the state attorney's office and request any information available on the rights of tenants in such conversions. Check your city's housing board for similar information, as well as your local citizen's housing action center, if there is one in your area.

Get the tenants of your building or complex organized into a group or association that can respond effectively to the sponsor's plans. Keep in mind that the owner or sponsor is out to make money—when the building or

complex is finally converted to condo or co-op status, the owner can liqui-
date his or her investment, realize a good profit, and go on to other things.
The tenants' key to a successful conversion is unity, so that everyone can
get the fairest possible deal from the sponsor. It's vitally important that the
tenants association hire an engineer to thoroughly inspect the premises and
submit a detailed report outlining the necessary repairs that must be made
immediately, and in the near future. The association should also engage an
experienced conversion lawyer who will negotiate price and terms with the
sponsor and will draw up a contract that protects the rights of all the tenants.

OTHER FACETS OF CONDO/CO-OP OWNERSHIP

MAINTENANCE. Unlike rental living, you as a condo or co-op owner are
responsible for the daily maintenance and upkeep of your unit. If a leak de-
velops in a faucet or pipe within your apartment, you must repair it. If,
however, there's a leak from the apartment above you or from the interior
walls, in most cases the building association or corporation must correct the
condition. They are also responsible for repairing any damage such as re-
plastering, if it is necessary to break through the walls in order to get to the
leaky pipe. Generally, however, the building association or corporation is
not obligated to pay for the redecoration of those walls. Check your proprietary lease or by-laws for further details.

INSURANCE. Insurance coverage in a condo or co-op development is fairly
evenly divided between the unit owner and the corporation or association.
Generally, the interior of your apartment or unit is your responsibility and,
as a homeowner, you should carry a comprehensive homeowner's insurance
policy. The corporation or association is responsible for the exterior of the
building or units and should carry sufficient loss and liability coverage for
this and the areas held in common.

THE MANAGEMENT COMPANY. The board of directors of a condo or co-
op often hire a real estate management company to oversee the smooth
functioning of the building or development, the hiring of employees, and the
handling of special problems that may come up from time to time. The
management company also collects the monthly maintenance fees, renders
expense and accounting reports to the board of directors, and acts as a li-
aison between the board and any outside agencies.

TAXES. As long as the condo or co-op is your primary or secondary residence, the Tax Reform Act of 1986 allows you to deduct the mortgage interest and, in the case of co-ops, the share of the corporation's mortgage interest that is included in your maintenance payment every month. You are also allowed to deduct your share of the building or development's property taxes. See chapter 28 for tax information regarding the renting or subletting of your unit.

GLOSSARY OF REAL ESTATE TERMS

Abstract of title a summary of the ownership history of a property, including changes in ownership, mortgages, liens, charges, etc.

Acceleration clause a stipulation in a loan agreement stating that the entire balance due will be payable immediately to the lender upon failure of the owner to meet periodic payments or other terms.

Access the means of approach to a property.

Acre a measurement of land totaling 43,560 square feet (4,840 square yards, 4,407 square meters).

Adjustable-rate mortgage (ARM) a mortgage loan agreement which provides that the interest rate will be adjusted periodically, based on a specified index.

Adjusted basis the cost of property plus closing costs and improvements minus depreciation claimed. Used to calculate taxable gain or loss on sale of a house.

Adjusted sales price the sales price of property minus commissions and other closing costs.

Agent an individual who has been given the power to act on behalf of another. A real estate sales agent is licensed by the state to work in affiliation with a real estate broker.

All-risk form the most widely used form of homeowner's insurance, including coverage for perils, except for a few specifically excluded. Also known as HO-3.

After-tax cost the true cost of owning a house after the reduction of personal tax liability has been considered.

Amortization the reduction of a loan balance by periodic repayments.

Appraisal   the examination of property by an outside professional for the purpose of estimating its current market value.

Appreciation   the growth in value of property over time as a result of increases in market value and demand.

Assessment   valuation of property for the purpose of taxation; a special-purpose tax.

Assignment   delegation of rights and responsibilities to another, such as a lessee in his or her relationship with a sublessee.

Assumable mortgage   a mortgage loan allowing the buyer of a property to take over the loan of the previous owner at the same interest rate and terms of the original mortgage.

Balloon mortgage   a form of financing calling for interest-only payments or payments with very little principal, with a large amount (or the entire balance) subsequently coming due in one installment.

Basic policy   a form of homeowner's insurance that covers certain named perils only. Also called HO-1.

Basis   for tax purposes, the buyer's cost of the house plus and minus adjustments; used for computing capital gain or loss.

Binder   a form of contract between a buyer and seller of real estate that specifies the main points in their agreement; to be replaced later with a formal sales contract.

Blanket mortgage   financing on more than one property under a single agreement.

Broad form   homeowner's insurance covering 18 named perils; also called HO-2.

Broker   an individual licensed by the state to represent sellers in real estate transactions directly or through agents and salespeople.

Buy-down   financing in which a developer arranges for the buyer to obtain a mortgage loan at below-market interest rate, with the developer subsidizing a portion of interest costs. In exchange, the price of the property probably is higher than that of comparable real estate.

Buyer's market   a market condition in which there are more sellers than buyers, forcing asking prices down in favor of the buyer.

Buyer's broker   a broker hired to represent the buyer's interests in a real estate transaction.

Cap   a ceiling placed on either the interest rate or the amount of monthly payments in an adjustable-rate mortgage.

Capital asset   property such as real estate, business assets, or investment.

Capital gain or loss   a gain or loss from the sale of a capital asset.

Cash flow   the availability of cash to an investor. "Positive" cash flow is a condition where more cash is being produced than is being spent.

Casualty insurance   part of a homeowner's insurance policy protecting property against loss from natural causes, acts of vandalism, and theft.

Closing   the final phase in a real estate transaction, when title is transferred from the seller to the buyer.

Closing costs   the additional expenses over and above the purchase price of buying and selling real estate.

Closing statement   a written summary of the transfer of title to real estate, showing the purchase and sales price, all closing costs, and the amount financed or transferred to the seller.

Collateral   security pledged for the repayment of a loan.

Commission   payments to an agent, broker, or salesperson for his or her services in the sale of a land, house, or other property.

Compound interest   the accelerating effect of savings when the interest earned is reinvested.

Comprehensive   the most expensive form of homeowner's insurance, with all-risk coverage; also called HO-5.

Condominium policy   homeowner's insurance that includes all-risk coverage but does not insure the building, designed especially for condominium owners; also called HO-6.

Consideration   usually a sum of money. In order to be binding, a contract must have consideration.

Contingency offer   a stipulation in a contract, such as the sale of a buyer's current house or agreement by the seller to perform repairs. The contract is not binding until the contingencies are satisfied.

Conveyance   the document, such as a deed, by which property is officially transferred.

Creative financing   arrangements to help home buyers afford payments or prices of houses and structured differently from traditional mortgage loans.

Credit report   an investigative report on a prospective buyer's credit history that is usually requested by a lender and completed by a credit bureau.

Declaration of homestead   a document filed with a county that protects all or part of a homeowner's equity from a forced sale.

Deed   the document used to transfer ownership of property from the seller to the buyer.

Deed of trust used in some states in place of a mortgage; the assignment of title to a lender until the entire loan balance has been paid.

Default failure to make mortgage loan payments when due, resulting in possible foreclosure on the property.

Default insurance often called *mortgage insurance*; a form of coverage lenders may require homeowners to carry and pay for. It will repay a portion of the lender's loan in the event of default.

Deferred gain a delay in tax liability allowed by tax law on income or profits such as profit on the sale of a house when another house is purchased or built within two years from the date of sale.

Depreciation the gradual decrease in market value of property, due to age, wear and tear, or market conditions.

Down payment the amount of cash, usually a percentage of the sales price, invested in property by a buyer upon entering a contract.

Earnest money deposit of money accompanying an offer to buy property, as a sign of good faith.

Easement the legal right to use or cross land owned by another person.

Equity the portion of a property's current market value representing the buyer's ownership, with the balance represented by the level of debt.

Equity conversion a term describing a reverse-annuity mortgage by which an owner or property accepts cash payments over time in exchange for a share of property ownership.

Equity line of credit available funds borrowed by a homeowner to be used at the homeowner's discretion. The amount that may be borrowed is usually a percentage of the homeowner's equity.

Escrow the temporary holding by a third party of deposited funds pending completion of a title search and the meeting of agreed conditions in a sales contract.

Exclusive listing an agreement between a seller and a broker that the broker be the sole selling and listing representative for a property transaction for a specified period of time.

Exclusion rule a once-in-a-lifetime provision allowing homeowners age 55 and older to realize up to a $125,000 gain on the sale of a principal residence without any tax liability.

FHA mortgage a form of financing in which a loan granted by a conventional lender is insured by the Federal Housing Administration.

FISBO a term describing a homeowner who sells property without the assistance of a real estate broker ("for sale by owner").

Fixed-rate mortgage   financing with a rate of interest that will not vary during the term of the mortgage loan.

Flexible-rate mortgage   an alternative term for adjustable-rate mortgage (ARM).

Foreclosure   the legal process of taking property away from a buyer because of failure to meet the payment terms of a mortgage.

Full amortization   the most common method of financing real estate, in which payments include part interest and part principal; the principal portion of each payment increases over the period of the loan.

General contractor   a professional builder or remodeling contractor who is responsible for completing a construction project directly and through hiring specialized subcontractors.

Graduated-payment mortgage   a form of financing with increasing payments over 5 to 10 years and a variable rate of interest.

Growing-equity mortgage   a mortgage with a fixed interest rate and extra payments to be applied directly to the principal.

Guaranteed loan   a form of real estate financing including a guarantee against default by the VA or FmHA.

Home inspection service   a diagnostic service performed by a contractor or experienced individual or company; the purpose is to point out defects or problem areas in properties.

Homeowner's insurance   insurance coverage protecting the homeowner from liability (damages to other people or property) and casualty (loss of or damage to a house or personal property).

Improvements   permanent additions to a house that increase its value.

Inflation   the increase in prices over time.

Index   a measurement of interest rates used to determine increases or decreases in interest charges in an adjustable-rate mortgage.

Insured loan   a loan granted by a conventional lender and insured against default by the FHA.

Interest   the cost of borrowing money from a lender.

Interest only   financing in which no principal is paid for a specified period of time.

Land contract   a form of financing in which the seller retains an original mortgage and title to the property until the loan is paid in full by the buyer.

Legal description   identification of a property that specifies its location and boundaries.

Lease an agreement between an owner of property and a lessee specifying a set amount of rent for a specified period of time.

Lease option a method of buying real estate in which a portion of periodic payments is applied to rent and a portion is used toward a down payment.

Lessee an individual who occupies property under the terms of a lease, a tenant.

Lessor an owner of property who contracts with a lessee under the terms of a lease, a landlord.

Leverage the use of borrowed money to purchase property.

Liability insurance a form of protection against claims resulting from injury to others or damage to the property of others.

Lien a claim against property in satisfaction of a debt, such as a mortgage, back taxes, etc.

Liquidity the availability of cash or of assets that can be converted to cash on short notice.

Listing 1) a contract between a seller and a real estate broker; 2) a property for sale.

Listing broker a broker carrying the original listing of the house, although other brokers may sell the property in a multiple listing situation; in that case, the original listing broker usually gets a larger percentage of the fee.

Loan origination fee a closing cost charged by the lender to process a mortgage loan; sometimes substituted for points and assessed on the same basis.

Long-term capital gain a gain from the sale of any capital asset that has been held for more than a specified period.

Long-term capital loss a loss from the sale of a capital asset that has been held for more than a specified period. Losses on personal residences are not deductible.

Low-rate mortgage a form of financing in which a large down payment is made, followed by a short period of payments with below-market interest rates.

Market value the current value of real estate that a buyer is willing to pay and a seller is willing to accept.

Mortgage a legal document between lender and purchaser stipulating the terms of repayment of a loan for a specific piece of property; a lien has been placed on the property.

Mortgage acceleration the process of paying off a loan more rapidly than required by the mortgage contract; a higher amount is paid to the principal each month.

Mortgage insurance any of three types of insurance based on mortgage balance and levels of payment: 1) mortgage life insurance pays off the mortgage balance in the event of a homeowner's death; 2) mortgage disability insurance pays the monthly mortgage charges when a homeowner is totally and permanently disabled; 3) mortgage default insurance is designed to pay a lender a portion of the outstanding balance of the loan in the event that a homeowner defaults.

Multiple listing agreement that allows property for sale to be marketed and sold by a number of brokers in addition to the original listing broker.

Multiple listing service (MLS) a real estate service that advises brokers of houses and other properties that are for sale.

Negative amortization a situation that can occur in adjustable-rate mortgages when monthly payments are insufficient to meet rising interest charges. As a result, the balance due on the loan increases rather than diminishes over time.

Notice to owner a document supplied to homeowners by contractors advising them of the state lien laws.

Offer a proposal to purchase property at a specific price and on certain terms.

Payment cap a provision in an adjustable-rate mortgage stipulating that monthly loan payments will not exceed a specified amount.

Personal property movable possessions, such as furniture, and not a permanent part of the premises.

Plat book a volume of maps of an area showing the location and boundries of properties.

Point an amount equal to 1 percent of the balance of a mortgage loan. Points are assessed by some lenders as a condition for making a mortgage loan. In effect, they are extra interest paid by the borrower at the outset of the loan.

Prepayment penalty a charge assessed against homeowners for early payment of a mortgage loan.

Principal 1) the amount actually borrowed in a mortgage loan; the portion of the amount that remains to be paid; 2) the major party to a real estate transaction.

Promissory note a promise to repay a loan.

Prorated expenses paid at the closing of a real estate transaction; property taxes and interest that are due to or from the individuals in the sale, divided according to the portion of the year each party will have occupied the house.

Property taxes   assessments paid by homeowners for schools, public works, and other costs of local government based on the assessed valuation of the property.

Proprietary lease   legal agreement from the co-op corporation that officially allows the buyer to occupy the co-op unit.

Prospectus   an official offering plan issued by condominium and cooperative sponsors which gives details of prices, location, and layouts of units, as well as procedures and regulations of the development.

Rapid-payoff mortgage   a form of financing with a fixed rate of interest and increased principal payments; also called a *growing-equity mortgage*.

Rate cap   a provision in an adjustable-rate mortgage stipulating that the rate of interest will never exceed a specified level.

Raw land   land plots that are undeveloped.

Real estate sales agent   an individual licensed by the state, who represents a broker in real estate transactions.

Real estate broker   an individual licensed by the state to represent homeowners in the buying and selling of property, either directly or through agents and salespeople.

Real property   land, buildings, improvements, and their permanent attachments.

Realtor   a real estate broker who is a member of the National Association of Realtors.

Reconveyance   the return of property rights to a homeowner upon satisfaction of a lien or debt.

Recording   the official entry of transactions, liens, and reconveyances into the permanent record of a county.

Red herring   term for the preliminary offering plan issued by sponsors of a condominium or cooperative conversion to tenants before the plan is officially approved by the state. Apartments cannot be sold from the "red herring" plan until the issuance of the formal prospectus.

Refinancing   the paying off of one mortgage loan by another loan for the same property.

Renegotiable-rate mortgage   also called a *rollover*; a mortgage with an agreed-on interest rate for a specified number of months or years. At the end of that period, the parties must agree on a new term and interest rate, or the loan will become due in full.

Rent option payment of a monthly sum of money of which part is for rent of a property and part is to be applied toward the purchase of the property.

Renter's insurance policy a form of homeowner's insurance that covers possessions and some improvements, but not the building itself, also called HO-4.

Replacement value a provision in a homeowner's insurance policy guaranteeing that, within limitations, losses will be reimbursed at current replacement costs.

Reverse-annuity mortgage (RAM) a form of equity conversion in which a homeowner accepts periodic payments from a lender. The payments accumulate as a loan to be repaid upon sale of the house within a specified period of years or upon the death of the homeowner.

Rollover a mortgage setting an interest rate and the amount of monthly payments for a specified period of time, to be renegotiated later; also called a *renegotiable-rate mortgage*.

Second mortgage a junior lien on property; a loan that has secondary claims in the event of default.

Seller take-back the seller's providing all or part of a buyer's financing on purchase of a property.

Seller's market a condition in which there is a plentiful supply of buyers and a limited supply of sellers of desirable properties. The effect is to raise the price of available properties.

Selling broker in a multiple listing property, the broker responsible for finalizing the sale. The selling broker may or may not be the listing broker.

Shared-appreciation mortgage an unusual financing arrangement in which the seller allows below-market rates and payments and in return is entitled to a share of the profits from sale of the property.

Shared-equity mortgage financing in which the down payment, monthly payments, and/or profits from sale of the property are split between the owner and another person or company.

Short-term capital gain a profit from the sale of a capital asset held for six months or less.

Subcontractor a specialist who is hired by a general contractor to complete a portion of a home improvement.

Subdivision a tract of land that has been broken up into smaller plots for future home sites.

Sublease an arrangement entered by a lessee of property in which a tenant makes payments to the lessee, who in return makes payments to the lessor.

Survey a measurement of the exact location and boundaries of a property.

Tax bracket also called the marginal tax rate; the percentage of a person's income that must be paid in income taxes.

Tax shelter an investment that allows an individual to avoid or delay a liability for income tax.

Teaser also called the *today rate*; a promise of low interest rates in adjustable-rate mortgages intended to attract buyers. The teaser is removed and a higher rate becomes effective within six months to two years.

Time sharing partial ownership of property, often recreational or vacation housing, in which the investor has the right to use the property for a specified portion of the year.

Title the proof of ownership.

Title insurance a type of protection insuring the homeowner against the consequences of a lien or encumbrance against a property that was not discovered during a title search.

Title search the process of examining the records to discover mortgages, liens, or claims against a property.

Transfer fee a closing cost for officially transferring the property from a seller to a buyer.

Unconditional lien release a document given to the homeowner by a contractor, freeing the homeowner from future liens of any suppliers or subcontractors.

VA mortgage a mortgage granted by a conventional lender and guaranteed by the Veterans Administration; also called a GI loan.

Variable-rate mortgage an alternative term for an adjustable-rate mortgage (ARM).

Variance an exception to local zoning regulations.

Warranty an assurance by a home builder of the quality and condition of materials used in a home for a certain length of time.

Wraparound mortgage a form of financing popular during times of high interest rates. The seller passes on to the buyer an assumable mortgage to a property. The buyer makes payments to the seller and, in addition, secures a new mortgage for the difference.

Zoning process that classifies real property for different uses, such as residential, industrial, or commercial. Zoning is usually strictly enforced by local governments.

INDEX

NOTES

NOTES

NOTES

NOTES

NOTES

NOTES

NOTES